Home-Based Mail Order

A Success Guide for Entrepreneurs

I would like to dedicate this book to my wife, Janet, my children, Greg and Christine, my mother, Mary Bond, and my late father, Charles Bond.

Thanks for your support and encouragement over the years.

Home-Based Mail Order

A Success Guide for Entrepreneurs

WILLIAM J. BOND

LIBERTY HALL
PRESS™

LIBERTY HALL PRESS books are published by LIBERTY HALL PRESS, a division of TAB BOOKS. Its trademark, consisting of the words ''LIBERTY HALL PRESS'' and the portrayal of Benjamin Franklin, is registered in the United States Patent and Trademark Office.

First Edition
First Printing

©1990 by TAB BOOKS

Printed in the United States of America

Library of Congress Cataloging-in-Publication Data

Bond, William J.
   Home-based mail order : a success guide for entrepreneurs / by William J. Bond.
     p.   cm.
   ISBN 0-8306-4045-2   ISBN 0-8306-3045-7 (pbk.)
   1. Mail-order business. 2. Home-based businesses. I. Title.
HF5466.B68 1990
658.8'72—dc20   89-39988
                                       CIP

TAB BOOKS offers software for sale.
For information and a catalog, please contact:

TAB Software Department
Blue Ridge Summit, PA 17294-0850

Questions regarding the content of this book
should be addressed to:

Reader Inquiry Branch
TAB BOOKS
Blue Ridge Summit, PA 17294-0214

Vice President & Editorial Director: David J. Conti
Book Editor: Joanne M. Slike
Book Design: Jaclyn J. Boone
Production: Katherine Brown

Contents

Introduction

WELCOME ABOARD. THANK YOU FOR CLIMBING ABOARD THE MAIL-ORDER express. This exciting express will take you into the wonderful world of mail order, and you can ride it without leaving your home.

You can own and run your own mail-order business. This book will show you how. It will show you how to succeed in your business, and how to develop the necessary technical skills and the right attitude. This book will show you how to gain the experience while starting part-time, and make your business succeed.

START YOUR BUSINESS AT HOME

Whether by choice or necessity, millions of Americans operate a business at home. Many start because they want to earn more money. The best action you can take today is to start your own mail-order business. A home-based mail-order business will give you an opportunity to use those special talents, abilities, and skills you have been developing all your life, perhaps in your job or career. It will give you a chance to show your excitement about your product or service to customers from all parts of the country and all over the world. Your office can be your den, your little-used family room, a room in the basement, or even a section of your attic. From your room in your home or apartment, you can build the foundation of your business, and you can make it grow.

GET EXPERIENCE BY STARTING PART-TIME

Many successful people in mail order continue with their present job and branch out their mail-order business on a part-time basis until they are ready for full-time. The key to success on a part-time basis is to do something *each day* for your mail-order business—even if you just look over your future advertisements, review your sales figures, or examine advertisements in other mail-order publications.

As the owner of a small mail-order business, you have an advantage: you can become close to the product and to your customers. The strong relationship with your customers will be very important in order to build your business and increase your income. You can gain experience by studying as many mail-order advertisements, seminars, books, and magazines as possible. This business, like any other, is constantly changing; it will demand constant education to keep you on top.

YOU CAN SUCCEED IN MAIL ORDER

You have the ability to succeed in this exciting and profitable business; however, *you* must believe you can succeed in order to do it. See your success in your mind first. You need no special education. Some successful mail-order owners are former clerks, secretaries, teachers, salespeople, piano tuners, carpenters, housewives, househusbands, production workers, engineers, and many other occupations as well. People from all walks of life can read and understand this book, and succeed in mail order.

Once you start your own business, you will begin a journey. This journey will change your life. You will stop thinking like an employee, and start thinking like an owner of a business. You will be your own boss. No one will tell you how to run your business. To start, all you need is the right information. The book you are now reading will give you all the information necessary to help you earn more money and build your business.

WHY IS THIS BOOK DIFFERENT?

Home-Based Mail Order is based on the latest developments in mail order and on my own experiences. I started my own mail-order business because I wanted to become my own boss. When I first started, my customer list was zero. After selecting my first product and advertising it, I started my journey and kept the journey going until I reached my destination of success. I now have a mailing list of over 30,000 people. My customers are from all over the country, from Maine to California, and all over the world, from France to China. My first product, a manual to help people start a newsletter, sold very well. Once my customers purchased one product from me, I developed an entire line of products. You can build a line of products as well. I run seminars on mail order. You can do the same in your business. Successful mail-order businesses build a line of products to help satisfy their customer's needs.

Home-Based Mail Order is different because it offers clear principles, techniques, and ideas to succeed in mail order. The book is taken from my own experience in the field, extensive research, and material I developed to run seminars about mail order. This book will be your personal seminar on how to start a mail-order business at home.

The mail-order business is the most natural business to start right at home, so you can stay with your family, avoid expensive rent for an office, and give yourself the flexibility of working at your own pace and setting your own hours. This book opens the heavy curtains, so you can move front and center and enjoy the best of two wonderful worlds: You can start your own business, and run this business at home.

DO THE EXTRA WORK

Remember the story about the woman who said, "The best, and coolest drink is from the deepest part of the well"? In mail order, you must be willing to keep looking, keep trying, and dig a little deeper to come up with the winner. Once you have a gut feeling about an idea, go with it.

Home-Based Mail Order gives you the mail-order basics, and the little-known ideas to help you earn more money. Many of my seminar attendees started their own mail-order businesses and now enjoy extra income and the potential to expand their businesses even more.

The book opens with step-by-step information on how to start your business at home, from the necessary business organization and permits to choosing the best working area. This book helps you choose the best-possible product to succeed in mail order. It will show you how to match your product to your target market: the people with the income and desire to buy from you. It deals with how to develop the best offer possible to make profits. It shows you how to write and place advertisements, and how to service your customers. It also shows you how to use free advertising, and how to expand your business using sales promotion techniques. Making the right management decisions and testing the important areas of your operation are included to keep you successful. The book winds up with an overall review of the most important principles of the business.

USE A SYSTEM

In order to succeed, you need a system. *Home-Based Mail Order* will give you the information you need to set up your system and make it work. An important part of the system is to select good mail-order products, and then develop the advertisements or sales material to sell them. You can sell services by mail, as well. A product is tangible, something you can see and touch—a piece of jewelry, for example. A service is work done for others. It might be serving as a consultant for others or a correspondence school to teach others about antiques. Nothing happens until a sale is made. You will learn the techniques to sell your products to the mail-order customers all over the world. Chapter 1 will discuss how to get started successfully.

1

You Can Make It
in Mail-Order

CONGRATULATIONS. YOU HAVE MADE AN IMPORTANT STEP UP THE LADDER OF opportunity with the purchase of this book. You have the ability to start and successfully build your own mail-order business. The book you are holding will give you the information you need to start.

There are a number of stories about how to become rich in the mail-order business. These stories talk about choosing one product, taking out one advertisement, and making so much money, you need a wheelbarrow to take it to the bank. This sounds so good, it would be nice to believe it. But the truth is that the mail-order business, just like any other business, is very difficult to master. It will take more than one advertisement; it will take proper planning, proper strategies, and proper management. This book will give you all the information about marketing and advertising you need to start and maintain a successful business at home. Although every business requires hard work, there are many rewards.

A THRILL THAT NEVER CEASES

As a mail-order owner, you will check your mail, and when you reach down into the mailbox, you will find mail addressed to you for your products or services. What a thrill! And this feeling never ends. As you open the envelopes, you will find checks, money orders, and bank checks made out to your company to purchase your products or services.

You can be the person who checks the mail, opens the mail, and deposits the checks at the bank. The one important advantage of the mail-order business is that you send the product only after you receive the order and the check. Most businesses require getting the order first, shipping it, and waiting for weeks, sometimes months, until the payment is made to you. Your mail-order business gives you the steady cash you need to keep the business going strong. You are in charge of your business, you are an entrepreneur.

THE ENTREPRENEUR

An entrepreneur defined is someone who is willing to take a risk, a person who is willing to invest his or her money, time, effort, and ideas to start, manage, and build a business into a profit-earning business. The entrepreneur can be a housewife, househusband, salesperson, teacher, retiree, small-business owner, professional, and so on. You can be successful by being alert, trying new things, and testing your results. Successful entrepreneurs take creative risks, they try new things, and they do the necessary work to make them successful.

Some entrepreneurs become millionaires. A recent study of millionaires found that many of them run their own business, some own their own mail-order businesses. If you work hard, choose the right product, and follow the directions in this book, you might also become a millionaire.

I enjoy the story of the two hobos sitting on a park bench in New York, watching the busy millionaires walking swiftly by to reach their offices. The hobo says, ''I would give a thousand dollars to be a millionaire like those people.''

As an entrepreneur many advantages are offered to you, such as being able to set up your own business and the freedom to do things your own way. You become your own boss. You free yourself from the office politics and apple polishing in many companies and organizations. You are the star in your own play. You are the key player and also the director of the full product.

However, just as advantages are given, there are some drawbacks as well. You will not have a boss to make decisions for you. You must rely on yourself. You must be willing to set realistic goals, and then work hard to reach them. You will succeed when you keep trying until you make things happen in your mail-order business. You can do it. This book will show you how.

WHAT IS MAIL ORDER?

Mail order is a method of doing business where you use the United States Postal Service as a major partner. For the cost of sending a letter, less using bulk mail, you can send your sales literature or advertising brochure to anyone—anywhere in the country. You can even mail your offers to people living in Europe, Asia, or anywhere in the world. You do not need a retail shop to sell your products or services. You can sell your products by mail, or by an advertisement in the newspaper, magazine, or even on radio and television.

Because all transactions are through the mail, you never come in personal contact with the customer. You sell by your sales letter or your advertisement in a mail-order magazine, the money is sent to you by mail, and you ship out the order as quickly as possible using the U.S. Postal Service, or another shipping or postal business.

In mail order there are two basic ways to reach customers. One is direct mail, the other is the two-step method which uses an advertisement to get the customers interested in your product or service. The direct-mail approach involves sending a sales letter, brochure, order card, and reply envelope to the customer and asking for the order. Remember, the customer is completely cold; he never heard of you, your company, your product or service prior to opening your letter. Direct mail is a very difficult and expensive way to do business in mail order. You purchase a list, print up the letters, brochures, and order cards, and pay the postage. Wait until your business is fully established before you venture into the difficult direct-mail method of mail order.

The two-step method uses a small advertisement in a magazine to inform your potential customer about your product or service. The advertisement asks the potential customer to send for more information, and when you receive their letter, you can then send them your full sales package. You can then send your sales letter, brochure, order card, and reply envelope.

The difference between the two methods is that, in the direct-mail method, the potential customer is completely cold; in the two-step method, the potential customer is warm; he or she showed an interest by sending for more information. Whichever method you choose, if your material works, you can attain a number of orders, and in the process build your mailing list. Your mail-order business will grow with a good mailing list to send your offers. Satisfied customers will make your business successful.

GETTING THE ORDER

You must sell to survive in the mail-order business. In order to sell, you must present your offer in an appealing way to the customer. What is the offer? It includes a good product, at the right price, with the right terms, at the right time. The offer is everything you present to the customer, from the advertisement in the magazine to the sales letter and order card. Your guarantee is also part of your offer. When you fully guarantee your products, the customer from the other part of the country will feel more confident ordering from you. Remember: the customer is looking at other offers besides your offer, so to get the order, your offer must be the best one.

BE A MAIL-ORDER BUYER YOURSELF

One of the first questions I ask in my mail-order seminars is: How many people buy products or services by mail? I am pleased when a large amount of the attendees raise their hands. I recommend you buy products or services by mail order while you start your own mail-order business. Find out how other mail-order sellers present, price, ship, and market their products. Even if you don't buy mail-order products, send for information about other products in your line. When you receive material from other mail-order owners, read it completely and keep a file of it for your records. I recommend that you keep files on many different areas such as new product and service ideas, notes from this book, classified advertisements, and advertising agencies. This information will be very valuable as you start and run your business.

You have been a customer for many years. What do *you* expect from a product? Just what conditions are necessary before you buy a product? Some customers look for a product that is unique, others look for price, still others look for how practical the purchase would be for them. Some customers will even send for information on your product, and then file it away for a later time. For example, I use the two-step method. Once I sent a customer some information about a newsletter manual. I never heard from him again. Even when I sent him other offers, I still didn't hear from him. Finally, years later, a check was sent to me for the manual, using an older price. I checked the date on the original offer and found that it was four years ago. I sent the manual to the customer giving him the former price. This customer had sent for the information, filed it away, and when he retired four years later, decided he wanted the manual and sent for it.

Most of your sales will be within a week or 10 days after you send the customer the information. Your customer will make a decision, and if the decision is in your favor, you will get the order. This is a real benefit about the mail-order business; you learn right away, within a week or two at the most, whether your offer is a success. When your offer is a success, you continue with it; when your offer falls short of your mark, you adjust it until it succeeds.

GIVE YOUR BUSINESS A PERSONALITY

Every business has a personality; your mail-order business is no exception. Once you select a product or service, commit yourself to it, and deliver it honestly and enthusiastically, you will develop an excellent reputation. I make it a habit in my mail-order business to give the personal touch to my customers. The personal touch means a personal letter thanking the customer for placing the order with you. It means shipping your product or service when you promised in your sales literature or your advertisement. For example, if you promised to ship in 10 days, do not wait for a full month to ship the product. You develop confidence rather than uneasiness in the customer if you deliver what you promise, when you promise.

Your customer purchased your product because he or she feels you have a special source of supply or position in the business. Get excited about the product and communicate this excitement to your customer. Your customer will sense this excitement in your sales material and advertisements—in all of your communications you send out a basic message. The best message you can send should be a positive, winning, upbeat attitude about your product or service. You must have confidence in your products and in yourself. One way to retain this strong confidence is to keep up with the latest developments in the mail-order business.

KEEP RESEARCHING TRENDS IN THE FIELD

Successful mail-order owners keep a close look at the field. For example, what mail-order products are being advertised on a regular basis? What mail-order companies run advertisements month after month, year after year? You can find many magazines at your local library. If your library cannot supply you with magazines, go to a large library in your area and use their magazines. If you cannot check them out, make copies of the mail-order advertisements that interest you. Make your own file of successful mail-order advertisements.

I like to look back at the last few issues of a mail-order-type magazine like *Popular Mechanics*, and then go back into the stacks, and review the last few years. I look for products and services sold by mail-order continuously. Why? A mail-order owner will continue to run advertisements when he or she is making a profit. Follow the successful advertisements, and keep up-to-date with the latest products and trends in the field.

FOCUS ON YOUR INTERESTS

Your chances of success are better when you choose products or services you have a real interest in—a special understanding or specialized knowledge. When you know something well, you can sell it better. Try to develop a narrow specialty. When you have a genuine interest in something, you can sell it better by mail order. Remember, you cannot hide your feelings. Your products and services become a part of you; you will be selling them week after week, month after month, and year after year. For example, Fred M. of New Hampshire made a success out of his hobby. He was very handy making wood objects in his basement workshop and specialized in making coffee tables out of pine wood.

Fred decided to turn his hobby into a profitable mail-order business. He advertised his products in furniture magazines and newspapers and received many orders. He developed a good following by selling a quality product, and by shipping the tables immediately after the sale. Fred is now selling his products to many furniture stores in his area.

Another successful mail-order owner is Maria T. of New Jersey. She enjoys making pottery and asked her husband to join her in the hobby. When they retired from their teaching positions, they started to sell their pottery by mail order. By selling their products by mail and including their products in new catalogs mailed twice a year, they have built a fast-growing business, run right out of their own home. Maria handles the paperwork for the business, while her husband handles the production side of the business.

Another successful mail-order business is selling information. Take the example of Bill V. of New Hampshire. He started a newsletter for computers a number of years ago. Bill was interested in the subject, so he wrote it himself. He built the business to 1,000 subscribers, and sold by mail order. His secret to success was writing a good newsletter with plenty of valuable information. It discussed the new products and changes in the field, and Bill continued to stay ahead of the competition.

Bill wanted to give his customers the most value for their money. By doing this, his customers continued to buy his service. He had competition, but the quality of his product and the good customer service kept his business growing, year after year. Bill turned the newsletter into a magazine, and sold it to a major magazine publishing company.

You have the potential to develop a product just like Bill and turn it into a winner. Develop a product based on your interests, and make it work.

CONTROL OF YOUR PRODUCT OR SERVICE

Bill had complete control of the newsletter service: he wrote the newsletter and sold it. Maria T. of New Jersey had complete control over her pottery business as well. Fred made his own coffee tables out of pine, and was able to keep the profits to himself because he didn't have to buy the tables from someone else. When you have control of your product, by making it, or writing it, or performing the services yourself, you become the source of supply. You are not obligated to buy from others. *You* control your business.

VISUALIZE THE BUYER OF YOUR PRODUCT

Many successful mail-order owners sell to both women and men with special needs. For example, Bill wrote and filled a need by offering his computer newsletter to people interested in computers before the market grew to the present competitive state. If you're interested in music, for example, think what products or services you could sell by mail order to a group of people also interested in music. One of my seminar attendees, Steve M. of Maine, started a mail-order business selling cassette tapes to retailers and store owners. He is presently doing a national mailing to reach retailers all over the country. He buys music, and turns out a product to reach a market he knows very well. Chapter 4 will give you additional information on establishing a market in your mail-order business. Think about the person to whom you want to sell. Think about where he lives, how he lives, what kind of work he does, the income he earns, the way he thinks, the future dreams, and his goals and aspirations. Become well acquainted with the special group you plan to sell to in your mail-order business.

WHY PEOPLE BUY BY MAIL

Billions of dollars are spent yearly by people who want the convenience of buying products and services at home. They want unique products—something different than what they see in the local stores. They want a bargain, and they want to get as much as possible out of their purchase. Give them everything they want, and they will come back and buy from you.

Always remember that you are selling an image. Give it to them. For example, a successful cosmetic firm owner once said, "I'm not selling chemicals or colors, I am really selling beauty, an image, a sense of attractiveness." Another example: when a customer buys a vacuum cleaner, they are not buying the metal, the wire, and the brush; they are buying the relief from doing the work by hand, the time they save from using the product, the attractiveness of their home, and a healthier home, free of dust.

Your customers and potential customers are buying your product for many reasons. Once you determine the key ones, you can develop a strategy to sell them. Once you find out why people buy your product, you can communicate to them by your mail-order literature. Chapter 6 will give you information to help you successfully communicate to your buyer.

BUILD A RELATIONSHIP WITH YOUR CUSTOMER

Successful mail-order owners build a relationship with their customers. Their customers expect certain things from the mail-order owner, and when the mail-order owner does all the important things right, a good relationship results. A good relationship will permit you to continue sending other products and service offerings in the future.

You can develop a relationship by making it easy for the buyer to purchase from you. A mail-order owner in Georgia, Fred T., who sells fishing supplies, uses easy-to-understand sales material and includes a stamp on the return envelope to help increase his returns. Fred uses a down-to-earth, homey writing style in his letters to customers, and works hard to make his message clear. Fred's business is growing more and more each year because he knows his customers and works hard to keep them buying over and over again.

REMEMBER THE GOLDEN RULE

You make money in mail order when you keep selling your customer. When you treat your customers squarely and honestly, they will treat you in the same manner. Treat others the way you would like to be treated. When a customer complains about your product or service, take steps to solve it right away. It takes a great deal of time to build a positive reputation, and a very short time to lose it. Solve your customers' complaints immediately. Send them a new product or send them their money back—do whatever is necessary to make things right.

MAKE YOUR PRODUCT LOOK GOOD

People buy products that appeal to them. Show the customer the benefits your product or service offers them. A customer benefit is anything contributing to improvement or advantage to your customer. For example, your product might make a person richer or happier or more relaxed, or it might even make him or her more attractive to the opposite sex. Give the reasons to buy your product and then ask for the order. Mail order requires good selling, and in order to successfully sell your product or service, you must ask for the order.

BELIEVE IN YOURSELF AND OTHERS

The way you run your mail-order business, and the promotional material you use, will reflect a message about you. Believing in yourself will have a positive effect on your business. People like to do business with someone who is positive and confident about his or her field.

Have confidence in your customers as well. Most customers are honest and reliable. I have received thousands of checks from customers from all over the world, and received only one or two checks with insufficient funds. People are basically good, and when you treat them right, they respond positively.

Now let's summarize the key points in this chapter. In the next chapter we'll discuss how to set up your home so you can start a mail-order business.

SUMMARY OF KEY POINTS

- You will enjoy seeing your mailbox full of orders and checks.
- An entrepreneur makes things happen.
- Mail order is a way of doing business. You never meet the customer face to face, but you must work hard to get the order.
- Nothing happens until you get the order.
- Consider becoming a mail-order buyer yourself.
- Develop a distinct personality in your business.

- Keep up with the new developments in the field.
- Sell a product or service you believe in.
- Take control of your product or service.
- Visualize the buyer of your product or service. Get to know the reasons people buy by mail.
- Make your product look good, the competition is rough in mail order.
- Stand tall, and believe in yourself and others.

2

Organizing Your Home
for Your Business

DURING MY SEMINAR ON MAIL ORDER, I ASK MY STUDENTS TO CHOOSE A ROOM, or a portion of their apartment, condominium, or home for their business. Many of my students already have a room or section of their home set up for that purpose. Working at home has become very popular in the past few years; there are 6 million people working out of their homes on a full-time basis, and 25 million people working at least 8 hours a week at home. The list on p. 12 lists the advantages and disadvantages.

There's no question that working at home is convenient, but the convenience is offset by the temptation to do errands, watch television, go to the local shopping mall, or talk with friends on the telephone. As Kay McHugh of Massachusetts, a mail-order owner of exercise equipment, said, ''I know I wasn't put on this earth to do errands. I try to spend as much time as possible on my business. I try to stay off the phone with friends during the day and run my own errands on weekends.'' Kay McHugh developed a system to keep her productivity high; she kept telling her family, friends, and others who wanted to take advantage of her time that she had her own work to do. Kay found that after the first six months, many of the interruptions slowed down, and she could focus in on her own priorities.

Advantages

- No commuting
- Convenience
- Save money for rental costs
- Tax advantages
- Spend more time with family and children
- Opportunity to share the business with family
- You become your own boss

Disadvantages

- Interruptions from family, friends, and others
- Isolation from business associates
- Difficulty in motivating yourself
- Lack of boss to tell you what to do

Kay is presently developing a list of previous buyers of her equipment so she can include them in her winter catalog. Kay set her business up in the basement of her ranch-style home, where she handles all her orders, prepares the sales material, and keeps all the records. She stores her equipment at a warehouse.

The exercise equipment business is a natural for Kay; she has been interested in exercise and dance since her mother took her to dance lessons at age 4. By working at home she can do something she has wanted to do all her life.

FIND A SUITABLE PLACE TO WORK

Setting up a formal work area serves as an excellent way to communicate to others that you are serious about your mail-order business. A formal work area is a separate area for you and your business—not one that you must share with other family members during working hours. For example, if you want to use the family room for your business, and your husband also wants to use the room for his hobbies, a great deal of friction may result. Choose a sufficiently large area where you can have some privacy and a feeling of professionalism. For example, Marge Smith of New Hampshire opened an office at home and picked a room next to her garage. Marge's room includes essentials such as a desk, files, a copy machine, and shelves for her books and supplies.

Janet Lupi from Ohio set up an office at home for her office supply mail-order business and picked a intermediate-sized area in her finished basement. Janet used some partitions to give her office privacy and to permit her family to use the family room at the same time. The partitions cut down on excessive noise. Janet added extra lighting to give her office a brighter look to prevent eye strain from insufficient lighting.

CHOOSE THE RIGHT CHAIR

You will spend a great deal of time in your chair. Make certain that it is comfortable, and that it will give you the necessary support. It must support your lower back—the area the bone doctor calls the *lumbar area*. The chair must be adjustable so your feet fall comfortably on the floor and your arms rest comfortably on the arms of the chair. Your chair should have easy rolling wheels or casters for greater accessibility around the office. Spend some time trying out your chair before you buy it. It must be right for you.

DESIGN THE OFFICE FOR PRODUCTIVITY

Most home offices are centered around the desk, and the most-used equipment or tools are located as close to the desk as possible. If you intend to use your personal computer in your business and your file cabinets regularly, you might want to move them closer to your desk. Make your equipment work for you, rather than vice versa. Draw up an office layout of your proposed office area, and then try the layout to see if it works for you. Change it or adjust it to make it work. For example, Paul Sine of Georgia, set up an office next to the laundry room in his ranch-style home. Paul needed some partitions to cut down on the excessive noise of the washer and dryer. Now that the partitions are installed, Paul can work with less noise and under less stress from the noise. Refer to Fig. 2-1 to use as a guide.

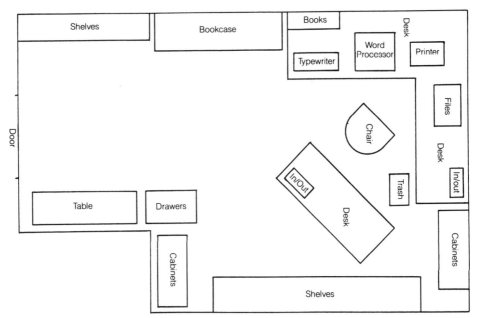

Fig. 2-1. This sample office layout is offered to give you ideas on some possibilities to turn your spare room, room section, basement, or attic into a comfortable, efficient office area.

COMPUTER OR TYPEWRITER?

Having a personal computer to use in your mail-order business will help you save time and money. If you don't have one, however, try to use a typewriter to communicate with your customers. You can purchase a typewriter at your local office supply company. Sometimes a good used typewriter is available. By using a typewriter, you will appear professional. Sending handwritten sales material to your customers will make you appear amateurish. Be sure to look professional at all times.

REQUIRED PERMITS AND LICENSES

Check with your local town clerk or city clerk to determine what permits are required to start your mail-order business at home. Many states require you to register your company name at the county clerk's office. If you use your own name for the business, for example, Francis Smith, this registration will not be required. Also, check the zoning ordinances in your area and make certain you can open a home business in your area. Spend the necessary time to cover all the necessary requirements, so you can legally open your business.

Your attorney will give you additional information on the necessary permits and licenses required to open your home business. Your attorney can also let you know how you can cover your personal liability, i.e., the amount of insurance you'll need to protect yourself if someone buys your product, and injures himself or gets sick by using it. Whether you need this insurance depends on your product or service.

HIRE AN ACCOUNTANT

You will need good records to show the costs, income, assets, and liabilities of your business. A good accounting system will help you achieve these results accurately. You will also open a checking account for your business; the account will use your business name on each check. Do not mingle the money from your personal checking account with your business account; keep each one separate. You will need the information from your checking account and your accounting records for your taxes at the end of the year. In the beginning of your business, you might find that you or a member of your family can handle the accounting.

When you hire help in your business, you add to your paperwork cost and your insurance costs. You will need W-2 forms, available from the Internal Revenue Service, for your employees. You will also be required to purchase workmen's compensation insurance to protect your employees. Hiring employees is expensive. Try to do most of the initial work yourself, or get help from members of your family. Once your business is well underway, you will be able to hire more help.

When you are ready to hire your first employee, write to your local Internal Revenue Service, and ask for Publication Circular E – Employee Tax Guide, a few copies of W-2 forms, and an application for your employment identification number. You will need this identification number to file your tax returns to the Internal Revenue Service.

PUT YOUR RESOURCES TOGETHER

You have a challenge before you. The challenge is to choose the room or area, and then put together the necessary furniture and tools to make it into a workable home office. Perhaps you can use a partition and use part of a room if space is a problem. You have the ability, the freedom, and the opportunity to set up your office, and get your mail-order business started. Joe Sugarman, one of the most successful mail-order owners in the country, started right out of his home. You can do it too. Let's look at how Joe did it.

A SUPERSTAR IN MAIL ORDER

Joe Sugarman, owner, president and founder of JS&A Group, Inc. of Chicago, started the business in the basement of his home. He calls his business one of selling products that think. Sugarman enjoys the mail-order business, and especially enjoys writing his own advertisements. He started the business in the early 1970s and his first product was a portable calculator. He ran his first advertisement in the *Wall Street Journal*, in February 1972. The price was $179.95, a high price at that time, before competition and production expertise brought the price much lower. Sugarman created the image of a very large company, even while he was working out of his basement. The first advertisement succeeded. Within ten days he earned $20,000.

Sugarman found that the more complete information he gave his customers, the more orders he received. His mail-order business grew so large that by 1973 he moved into a new facility to handle his growth. In this book we will discuss how you can develop a successful business, too, right out of your home.

STATE SALES TAXES

Each state has different regulations for state sales taxes. Contact the state sales tax bureau and inquire about the specifics in your state. State regulations differ from state to state. For example, in Massachusetts, if you sell a mail-order product to a customer within the state, you will charge a sales tax; however, if you sell to a customer outside the state, no tax is charged. This sales tax is paid on a monthly or quarterly basis.

CHOOSE THE BEST BUSINESS ORGANIZATION

You can choose a *sole proprietorship*, whereby you supply the capital and receive all the income and the losses. In a sole proprietorship you have all the personal liability, which means you may assume the responsibilities of your losses, and you must supply the capital. This is the easiest business to start.

Some small business owners decide to start a partnership with someone who can add expertise and capital to the business. A partnership is an agreement by two or more people, and must be in writing, preferably by an attorney. The contract should include partners' names, addresses, duties in business, investments, how profits will be shared, how losses will be shared, and under what conditions the business can be terminated. Try to make certain that the contract covers all possible situations—people and situations change in any business over a period of time.

Another business organization to help you increase capital and add to the list of owners is the corporation. This is the most formal business organization. It requires a charter from your state, you must select a board of directors, and also select officers and issue shares of stock. A stockholder can only lose the amount of money he or she invested in the stock. Stockholders share in the profits based on their stock holdings. These profits are not as high as in the partnership and the sole proprietorship form of business. Check with your attorney to select the best business organization for you. Now let's summarize the chapter.

SUMMARY OF KEY POINTS

- Working at home is difficult. It may be convenient, but avoid the temptation to do other things, such as errands, or watching television to escape your mail-order obligations.
- Choose the best location for your office.
- Choose a quality chair and design the office around it for productivity.
- Use a computer to save time and money. If you decide not to use a personal computer, use a good typewriter to communicate to your customers.
- Obtain the required permits and licenses for your home mail-order business.
- Check with your attorney about the legalities of your business, and your personal liabilities.
- Ask an accountant to set up an accounting system.
- The Internal Revenue Service will supply you with the necessary forms, applications, and information you need for tax purposes.

- Check the regulations on sales taxes in your state.
- Choose the best business organization possible.

3

Choosing the
Best Product

NOW THAT YOU HAVE SET UP YOUR HOME OFFICE, IT'S TIME TO DECIDE ON THE best possible product or service for your customers. When choosing, you must consider the customer. A wise mail-order operator remarked, "A product is made for a customer. A customer is not made for a product." Keep this important principle in mind in your product selection process. Your product or service should be customer-oriented.

HOW DO LARGE COMPANIES SELECT THEIR PRODUCTS?

Large companies choose products only after they've done extensive research and have a clear feeling that there are enough people to purchase the product. For example, a large toiletries company spent millions of dollars on a new underarm deodorant. They spent such a large amount on this product because they knew they were dealing with a market of billions of dollars.

Another method large companies use is the focus group. This group is a carefully selected group of people who examine and use the product in carefully observed conditions. For example, did the people open the product correctly? Did they use the product correctly? Did they speak favorably about the product? Did they use it in a different way than we intended in the first place? Based on the results of many focus groups, products are changed, modified, and adjusted to meet the needs of the customer.

You can use the focus group concept by watching people shop in retail stores or in a trade show. Your product or service must attempt to satisfy the wants and desires of the customer. To achieve this you can do a product benefit analysis to determine the benefits the customer will receive from your product. Refer to Fig. 3-1. Notice the specific benefits for this product. Benefits will help you sell the product.

CLASSIFY YOUR PRODUCT

There are three types of products sold today. The first group includes convenience products such as cigarettes, candy, costume jewelry, milk, and other products that can be purchased quickly and conveniently, without much thought and little consideration for price. Convenience products are not good mail-order products because people feel these products are easiest to purchase in many retail locations.

The second product classification are shopping goods, which requires the customer to spend time shopping and comparing before they buy. Examples of shopping goods are cameras, tape recorders, VCRs, or a special dress or coat. The price, color, style, and features are important to the consumer of this product.

The last classification is the specialty good, whereby the consumer makes a decision based on the brand name of the product. Designer jeans would be an example of this specialty classification, and the consumer will travel or buy from a mail-order seller if this product is offered. Another example is the golf-equipment manufacturer who sells his equipment not at retail stores, but only at pro shops at golf courses. Specialty products make good mail-order products. Review your product to determine the correct classification for it.

DEVELOP A PRODUCT IDEAS FILE

Product ideas come and go. A successful product must be carefully researched to make it pay off in profits. In my seminars, too often students talk about product ideas and never go beyond this stage. You can get product ideas by purchasing mail-order products. Use it, taste it, check the quality, check the mailability and attractiveness of the product. Another excellent way to develop product ideas is to go to your local library and spend a few hours looking over classified and display advertisements in magazines. Some very popular mail-order-oriented magazines are *Popular Mechanics, Income Opportunities*, and *Salesman's Opportunity*. Look for products and services advertised over and over again. Some products are sold month after month, year after year, decade after decade. One prime example of this is the Charles Atlas fitness course that sold in various magazines for many years. The course stressed the benefits of being strong and with the skills developed from the course, the customer could know

Product-Benefit Analysis

Product ____Men's Dress Shirt_____

Brand _____Lot #703_____

Date Completed __5/7/--___ Completed By ___Pat Johnson___

PRODUCT

Feature	Advantage	Resulting Benefit
1. Polyester-cotton blend fabric	1. Wrinkle-free fabric	1. No ironing, more leisure time
2. Body-fit style	2. Cut to fit	2. Neat appearance
3. Button-down collar	3. Collar stays neat	3. Stylish appearance
4. Arrow brand	4. Well-known brand	4. Assurance of quality
5. Pastel colors	5. Complementary colors	5. Versatility-wear with different colors
6. Double-stitched seams	6. Longer wear	6. Economy

BUSINESS

Feature	Advantage	Resulting Benefit
1. Location	1. Smith Mall	1. Easy to get to-saves time
2. Hours	2. 9 a.m.-9 p.m. 7 days/week	2. Shop at customer's convenience
3. Credit terms	3. 30 day open account, Visa and Mastercard	3. Have the merchandise now, pay for it later
4. Product lines carried	4. Leading name brands	4. Assurance of quality
5. Quality of salespeople	5. Well-informed about merchandise	5. Provide information which helps customer make effective buying decisions
6. Advertising	6. Frequent, informative advertisments	6. Provide info. which helps customer make effective buying decisions

Fig. 3-1. You are selling a great deal more than a men's dress shirt. You are selling neat appearance and style, with wrinkle-free fabric. The more advantages and benefits your mail-order product offers, the greater your chances to sell to today's mail-order buyer.

"how the 97 pound weakling can kick the sand into the bully's eye on the beach." Choose a quality product you believe in—one that is unique and one you can sell at the right price to make a profit.

Use the space provided below to jot down your product ideas. Visualize the customer and then choose something to meet his needs. For example, if you want to sell a product or service designed for the elderly, spend some time talking, listening, and observing the group to get product ideas. Get to know this market. One of my students in a mail-order seminar worked in a rest home, and from this experience, she developed a number of product ideas. Perhaps you have some experience that lends itself to specific product ideas.

Product/Service Ideas

_____   _____

_____   _____

_____   _____

_____   _____

_____   _____

_____   _____

_____   _____

Once you get some product ideas, narrow them down to a few and then do your research on them. For example, find out the manufacturer, the price, size, color, shipping costs, and information on how the product is being sold today. You can find a listing of all manufacturers at your public library. Gather all the information possible on your product; become an expert on the product.

WHAT IS THE BEST POSSIBLE MAIL-ORDER PRODUCT?

It's a good idea to choose a product that everyone needs—a product that both women, men, and children will buy over and over. Remember: Your product is made for people. When you spend the necessary time and effort, you will come up with some excellent ideas. Here is a list of the best possible principles of your mail-order product superstar:

- It looks attractive.
- It is unique.
- It has excellent features.

- It is easy to mail.
- It can be used by a broad section of the population.
- It can be used by young, middle age, and older people.
- It does not break or melt.
- It gets used up, requiring another purchase.
- It is easy to store.
- It offers important benefits to the customer.
- It can make a profit for you.
- It is needed by a special group.
- It can be a good lead product to sell other products.

Using these guidelines gives you some valuable ideas of the necessary ingredients for a good mail-order product.

SINGLE OR MULTIPLE PRODUCTS

You must determine if you want to sell a single item such as a book or electronic calculator or use this as a lead product to sell other products over and over again. The ideal mail-order business sells a good-quality lead product and then keeps selling other products to go with it. This happens all the time in everyday life: you purchase a pair of shoes, and while standing at the counter, the salesperson tries to sell you shoe polish, water protection lotion, stockings, shoestrings, handbags, and other products to go with the shoes. It is very difficult to build a mail-order business with the one-shot or single product. Success and profits result from selling your hard-earned customer over and over again.

DEVELOP YOUR OWN MAIL-ORDER BUSINESS PERSONALITY

When you select a product, also consider whether or not the product blends into your business. For example, if your first product is an informational manual on careers for the business school graduate, you would not want to sell the next manual on how to shop for antiques in New England. Develop a clearly defined personality to help your customer look to you for products and services in a particular field. At the right time add another manual on new careers in the twenty-first century for business school graduates. Offer a line of quality products that expands to meet the changing demands.

OTHER PRODUCT SUGGESTIONS

Almost everything can be sold by mail, from Christmas trees to correspondence courses to fresh tropical fruit. Refer to the list on p. 24 for additional ideas.

Some Mail-Order Products/Services

- Gifts
- Tools
- Cookbooks
- Clocks
- Home improvement items
- Small appliances
- Knitted goods
- Toys
- Christmas trees
- Chain earrings
- Floating hearts
- Automobile aids
- Miniature pinball games
- Stovetop broilers
- Unique stuffed animals

- Jewelry
- Clothing
- Reminder service
- Inspirational books
- Automobile tire pumps
- Baseball cards
- Flower seeds
- Satin sheets
- Sunglasses
- Rope chains
- Automobile polish
- Weight reducing aid
- Exercise training aid
- Leather slippers
- Sewing kits

- Correspondence courses
- Collection service
- Information services
- Unique posters
- Decorator tray plaques
- Paint sprayers
- Hairpieces
- Address labels
- Religious charms
- Wall murals
- Paint strippers
- Self protection devices
- Glove liners
- Knitting kits

There are many more. This is just a small list to get you started. Choose a product that you would buy by mail. Choose a product that has a good market. One successful mail-order owner said, "People are interested in three things, sex, money, and diet." Choose a product that is of interest to people.

GO TO TRADE SHOWS

Many ideas are developed by mail-order owners by going to trade shows. Many products and services are displayed at these shows. Mail-order products always look better when the product is being used. Keep this in mind when you choose your product. For example, there are many gift shows where manufacturers or distributors are available to explain the features and discuss the advantages of their product. Spend time reviewing the product of interest to you. Watch the booth to see the amount of people inquiring about the product.

Trade shows offer quality products and services to start your product selection process and keep it going. You will also find out how many products are sold and whether they are sold by mail, magazine, radio, television, or some other means. At these trade shows you will receive a tremendous amount of written information on the various products and services. Take this information on the products or services that are of interest to you and read it later. After reading the information on the products or services, you may want to write to the companies that offer products or services you would like to sell by mail order. The only way to get a good product is if you *read* and *learn* about the product and about the company that manufactures the product. When you decide to write to the company, ask them questions about the product. Get as much information as you need to make a decision about taking their product on.

OTHER SOURCES

Use your Chamber of Commerce. The Chamber of Commerce is a voluntary association of businesspeople to help promote the business atmosphere of the town or city. Each Chamber of Commerce provides different types of services, depending upon their size and location, but almost all Chambers provide excellent economic statistics on their communities. Use this valuable information.

The U.S. Department of Commerce assists businesses in expanding their foreign and domestic trade. They have extensive libraries and publications that are available to you. They also provide valuable advice and marketing studies, information on new products, census data, and general economic information. The U.S. Department of Commerce also publishes a very important and necessary publication called the *Commerce Business Daily*. This excellent listing tells the businessperson what the U.S. Government is interested in buying and selling. The *Commerce Business Daily* can be an ideal source of information when you are trying to choose a product. You know the products have an excellent chance of success right away when the U.S. Government is interested in purchasing them and spends billions on products and services yearly. Be sure to take advantage of the many free sources of information available to you from the federal government.

Look for new products in the various magazines and trade journals available to you. Your public library has many magazines in stock, and some libraries even loan out magazines and journals to be taken home for a week or more. Look for magazines that have shopper's sections in which products are advertised, often with a photograph and description of each product, the name of the company, and the cost of the product. These shopper's sections are very good sources of new product ideas, and at the same time, you can get the names of companies selling the products.

Visit stores for new product ideas. If you would like to sell a product to be used by the hobbyist, visit all the hobby shops and major stores that supply hobby equipment. You might write to local hobby stores. Ask them to send their catalog on hobby equipment. Major catalogs like Sears and Roebuck are also excellent sources for product ideas.

Use the Small Business Administration of the United States Department of Commerce. Many new mail-order businesspeople have successfully sold their new products by using the many booklets and information supplied by the Small Business Administration of the United States. One booklet, called "Developing and Selling New Products," gives you a list of new products developed, the name of the company (or person) that originally conceived the idea, and the company that finally manufactured the product for sale to the public. There are many Small Business Administration field offices located in major cities all over the country. If you would like to take advantage of the many services such as loans, management assistance, courses, conferences, workshops, clinics, publications of management, and business information, write to the *Small Business Administration*, Washington, DC 20416. Ask them to put your name on their mailing list for future publications and services.

In the final analysis you have to make the decision on what product you would like to sell by mail order. You should choose a product that you:

- feel comfortable selling
- know very well
- believe has a good chance of selling profitably by mail order
- feel very strongly about
- believe will last in the competitive mail-order business

Now that you have found the right product to sell by mail order, the next logical step is to find the most dependable source of supply for your product.

HOW TO FIND SUPPLIERS

As a beginner in mail order, you must first find a supplier or suppliers that will sell you the quantity you need to get started in the mail-order business. Here are some of the factors you must consider in choosing your supplier:

- What is the price?
- What is the waiting period?
- What are the quality standards?
- What extra services does this supplier have that will be beneficial to you?
- Is the supplier reputable?
- Do you know any of the customers of this supplier?
- Will the supplier give you any professional references, such as attorneys, accountants, banks, Chamber of Commerce, or their suppliers?

These are just a few of the many questions you must ask yourself before you decide on a particular supplier of your product.

You can find many suppliers right in the yellow pages of your local telephone book. If you cannot find a supplier in your area, the local library will have a supply of various yellow page directories. You should try to get a supplier as close to your area as possible; this will help you to save money on shipping costs. In addition, the reference librarian at your public library has a book called *List of Manufacturers*. This book offers information on products, product lines, how to purchase, whom to contact, along with addresses and telephone numbers.

Once you settle on three or four potential suppliers, ask them to give you a bid on a certain quantity of your product. You will find that the bids may be very different depending upon the size of the supplier, the automation of his company, and the supplier's knowledge of the business. Once you get the bids in from all the suppliers, the two items you must consider are the price and the time of delivery. You want to get the very best price possible in order to make the most profit. You also must have the products on time in order to get them in the mail to your customers. There is nothing more frustrating to your customer than waiting for delivery of his product, especially when he has already paid for the product.

If you choose a supplier that is located in a distant part of the country, there will be shipping charges to pay, which will cut into your profits. *You* must be the final decision-maker on what supplier will be best for you. Although one supplier charges a slightly higher price, the supplier might offer a particularly high-quality product and have a good line of products. Such factors will help your mail-order business grow.

Once you decide on a certain supplier, check on his references, such as his bank or accountant, to be sure that the supplier has a good solid reputation. If you know any other businesspeople who are doing any business with this supplier, talk with them to get additional information about the supplier.

A good supplier is vital to your business and must provide a quality product to sell to your customers. For this reason, establishing a solid relationship with your supplier is very important. To create a good, healthy, strong and reputable business, you have to be loyal to the supplier and the supplier must be loyal to you. Your supplier needs your business in order to run his business; you need your supplier to successfully run your business. It's important to work together as a partnership.

BE A MATCHMAKER

You can be successful if you *match* your carefully researched product with your market. By bringing the two together you will have a winner. For example, a mail-order owner in Pennsylvania has sold men's shoes and slacks for years to customers from all over the country who expect quality, correct fit, and a reasonable price. The first sale is essential; you must convince the customer your product or service will satisfy his or her needs. Once you complete the sale and prove to the customer your product or service is worthwhile, you have a customer who has the potential to keep buying from you for years. Your secret to success is matching your product to your market with persistence and continuing research.

SUMMARY OF KEY POINTS

- Your product or service should reflect your personality, interest, and knowledge. The more you know about a product the more enthusiastically you can sell it to others.
- Classify your product according to either a convenience, shopping, or specialty product.
- Consider the benefits of your product or service.
- Try to answer these basic questions:
  - —What does it do?
  - —Why should I ask people to buy it?
  - —How will it benefit others?
  - —Keep a product ideas file and keep it up to date.
- Keep in mind the essential elements that will add to your product's appeal (for example, it can be used by both men and women, and it can be sold over and over again).
- Choose a good single product and turn it into a lead product.
- Review the mail-order products listed in this chapter.
- Attend trade shows to gather ideas and establish a relationship with a supplier.
- Use the services of the Small Business Administration.
- Choose your products, services, and suppliers carefully.

4

How to Connect
with Your Customer

NOW THAT YOU HAVE SELECTED THE PRODUCT OR SERVICE, YOU CAN MATCH IT TO the best possible customer. Some people think that once they start their own business, they will get customers very easily. In mail order your customers are called your *market*. A market is the total demand of the potential buyers for your product. For example, if you sell a product for artists by mail order, and your research shows there are one million artists in the country, your basic market is one million people. The more you know about your market, the more likely you will be to reach them in your mail-order business.

A *target market* is a particular group of people with particular abilities, needs, and desires. Your market might be teachers, sports fans, business owners, bird watchers, carpenters, working women, or police officers. You want to direct your activities to hit the target market directly. Get to know as much as possible about the target market. Think about your market. Who is he or she? Where does he or she live? How much does he or she earn? What is his or her occupation? The answers to these questions will determine how you will advertise your product. For example, if you are selling Indian jewelry, who will be interested? Where are they located? What magazine reaches this specialized market? You want to hit your target market directly, just like a shooter at a rifle range wants to hit the target directly on the bull's-eye. Try to match your product to your customer as closely as possible.

DO YOUR HOMEWORK

Your main goal is to learn the demographics of your customers. *Demographics* are the tangible specifics of your customer, such as age, sex, and race. The list below shows what demographics include. Use the space provided to jot information on the demographics of your customer list.

Writing good advertisement copy and developing an exciting offer will require a clear understanding of the demographics of your market. For example, if your market is between the ages of 25 and 35, their available income to buy your gift product would be more than if your market is between the ages of 65 and 75. The age and the income are very important considerations when you sell to your market. Write an estimate of the various demographic segments listed below. This will give you a more accurate view of your customers.

A Sample of Demographics

1. Age _____

2. Sex _____

3. Income _____

4. Occupation _____

5. Race _____

6. Education _____

7. Geographic
   Location _____

YOUR CUSTOMER GOES THROUGH CYCLES

Your customer will buy your product if the product is something he or she needs, has appeal, and is affordable. For example, Greg Smith, a 19-year-old attending college in California, will spend most of his income on his education or his hobby. Your mail-order product must appeal to him to spend his limited income during his college years. After Greg graduates from college and enters the business world, he will have more income to buy many products and services. Businesses are trying to reach people between the ages of 23 and 44 because of their high income and because the largest portion of the 250-million population in America is in the 23 to 44 age group. In addition to age and income, a person's marital status will effect what he or she buys. Be sure to examine *all* the demographics of your target market and use them in your mail-order advertising.

Psychographics takes into account the lifestyles of your customers. These statistics are used by more and more mail-order owners because they offer additional information about the customer. Psychographics encompass the way a person lives and the type of personality he or she possesses. The outgoing person who spends a great deal of time entertaining others will buy certain household products and gift products that a quiet, home/family-type person would not buy. An understanding of the personality and lifestyle of your consumer will help you place your product or service in the consumer's mind and make it attractive to him or her.

In your mail-order business your main goal is to get a share of your market. You get a share of the market when they buy your product rather than your competitor's product. The best way to increase your share of the market is to know your customer and attend to the needs of your market.

BE SENSITIVE TO YOUR MARKET

The best mail-order owners know their market and they are sensitive about their market's needs. For example, I remember an important comment from a mail-order owner, Jack Worth of Cleveland. He said, "Sorry, I cannot buy certain products for my customers. They expect the highest quality product available, and I'm afraid this product does not live up to our standards." Get to know your customers, not only through demographics, such as age and income, but also through psychographics, such as attitudes, lifestyles, and opinions. Get to know your market like a family member. Being sensitive to your customer permits you to serve them better.

THE MAIL-ORDER CUSTOMER BILL OF RIGHTS

Your customer is important to your success. Always remember, the customer has rights. Each market has specific needs, but *all* markets have rights which include the following:

1. The right to expect quality merchandise or service from you.
2. The right to complain and return shoddy or defective merchandise.
3. The right to expect the mail-order owner to attend to a complaint.
4. The right to expect honest and reliable mail-order advertisements.
5. The right to expect the mail-order owner to guarantee the product or service.
6. The right to take a complaint or disagreement to the owner or the top management of the seller.
7. The right to expect the mail-order seller to listen to complaints and make the necessary corrections for future customers.
8. The right to expect a full cash refund promptly when making a return.

9. The right to be treated as a customer, not an enemy.

Today's customers are smart, difficult to satisfy, and want to be treated fairly. If you fail to live up to the terms you offered in your advertisement or sales literature, the customer may send a complaint to the Better Business Bureau and may even contact the Federal Trade Commission. Customers get very nervous when goods are not shipped within the terms stated in your advertisement or sales literature. If you state shipment within 7 days, make certain you do it. The Federal Trade Commission requires that all mail-order goods be shipped within 30 days of the receipt of the order, unless a later date was specified in the advertisement, or the buyer must be given a cash refund. When there is a delay, keep in touch with your customer.

STAY CLOSE TO YOUR CUSTOMER

To offer your customer the best product and the best offer available will require your constant attention. Your customer never stays the same, he or she is constantly changing. You can attain information from your customers by asking them questions or talking to them over the phone; however, the best way to keep current is to stay close to your customer. When your customer has a problem, solve it as soon as possible. When you show an interest in your customer, it will show you care enough to do more. Be willing to do a little more than your competition. For example, Joe Sugarman, the mail-order expert discussed earlier, wrote a large advertisement titled "The Truth about Pocket Calculators" and listed specific information about calculators, such as price, display, choosing a size, and where to buy, so that his customers could buy with more confidence. The advertisement was one of the firm's most successful calculator advertisements. Joe researched his market and then developed an outstanding advertisement to get a share of the market.

A president of a New England college asked her research department to do a profile on the day students at the institution. The report showed the reasons for attending, place of residence, means of transportation, work, income, formal education, interests, and goals. The report was given to the faculty and staff at the college, so they would get to know the students and tailor their curriculum to students' needs. In your mail-order business strive to develop a profile of your customers to serve them better.

MARKET DATA AVAILABLE TO YOU

There are two sources of information. The first one is *primary data*, which includes data collected for the first time to solve a specific problem. *Secondary data* is previously collected data. Secondary data includes many free or inexpensive sources from the federal government, such as annual survey of manufacturers, census of manufacturers, census of population, and census of retail trade, wholesale trade, and selected service industries. Secondary data includes magazines, books, research data from research companies, and information available from numerous governmental agencies such as the Small Business Administration and the Department of Commerce. These important sources are listed for you in Appendix B. Take advantage of the wealth of information available to you free from your federal, state, and local governments.

ONE MARKET OPENS UP OTHER MARKETS

Melvin Powers, a mail-order owner and consultant from California, sold psychology books by mail order. He developed a catalog to display the books for his customers. Melvin started his business selling to the general public—then to psychiatrists, nurses, chiropractors, and eventually to universities, colleges, and public libraries. Thus learning one market will open the door of opportunity to other markets.

Choose a market you feel comfortable with and be ready to move into other markets. Take the example of Lynn Gordon of New Hampshire. She developed a unique table lamp and sold it by mail order out of her own home. When the business started, Lynn was selling to the general public. Now the bulk of her business is the wholesale business. Lynn sells to large wholesalers who sell to lamp retailers. Lynn is building her mail-order list and increasing the sales and profits in her business.

INMATES AS A TARGET MARKET

A mail-order firm in Massachusetts is sending their catalogs to a captive market: the inmates in the state's penal institutions. The inmates enjoy the opportunity to select from many products, including clothing, radios, and television sets. Just what products they can purchase and have delivered into the jail varies from one institution to another. The inmates enjoy the opportunity to purchase for themselves, especially for the holidays, and this market is growing faster and faster.

The important point here is to look at your target market in a different way. What group of people would be happy to buy your product or service? What about the patients at a long-term health care hospital? How about the patients at the nursing home in your area? How about the college students of America or the service men and women of America? The list goes on and on along with your imagination.

TARGET MARKET IDEAS

There are hundreds, even thousands, of markets for your product. For example, Joseph Mancusco of New York developed a cassette tape for entrepreneurs and businesspeople who wanted to expand their businesses. Joe is now running a huge mail-order business selling many products and services to this special group. Refer to the list below for markets you might want to consider for your product. Remember that your choice of a market with the income need, and desire to buy is essential to success in mail order. Look for a market that has the potential to grow in the next few decades.

Markets

- Mail-Order Owners
- Gift Store Owners
- Small-Business Owners
- Working Women
- Engineers
- Accountants
- Teachers
- Writers
- Left-Handed People
- Handicapped People
- Nurses
- Doctors
- Buyers of Business Books
- Seminar Attendees of Stress-Management Seminar
- Insurance Salespeople
- Computer/VCR Owners

- Home Economics Teachers
- Business Colleges
- Chemical Engineers
- Civil Engineers
- Farmers
- Printers
- Publishing Houses
- Manufacturers
- Convenience Stores
- Guidance Counselors
- Do-It-Yourself Market
- Gourmet Cooks
- Graphic Artists
- Lawyers
- Salespeople in Computer Field
- Expensive Jewelry Buyers

Many markets are available on mailing lists that you can rent from a mailing-list company. These markets can be reached by specific magazines. For example, if you wanted to reach writers, there are two major magazines: *The Writer Magazine*, and *Writer's Digest* magazine. By placing an advertisement in one of these magazines you can reach 200,000 to 300,000 writers.

Once you know your market completely, you can find other ways to reach them. We will discuss this in more detail in a later chapter.

The Business Owner Market

Business owners must buy a number of products for their businesses and many offer gifts to their customers. Some mail-order owners sell calendars and desk diaries to help the business owner with planning and scheduling. The business owner market is ideal because business owners purchase products and services that are required 7 days a week, 52 weeks a year. One very successful mail-order owner from California devotes his business to selling office products to businesses. Keep your product quality high and the prices reasonable to reach the business owner.

The Career Woman Market

Millions of women are not only moving in jobs with more and more responsibility, but are earning better salaries as well. The career woman is so busy she lacks the time to spend shopping for herself. You might want to pursue this important market with products such as books, correspondent courses, video tapes, gifts, jewelry, clothing, and toys.

The Do-It-Yourself Market

The cost of repairing the leaking faucet or the noisy washing machine has increased enormously during the past few years. Many homeowners would rather attempt to fix a leaky faucet themselves than pay the plumber $150 to $200 to fix it. You can serve this market if you can develop an easy-to-understand plan to repair a leaky faucet.

People will buy information if it helps them save time and money. One of my friends, Greg Johnson of Massachusetts, is an appliance repair person for a large appliance retailer. He attended one of my mail-order seminars and decided to develop a small book on how homeowners could fix their own appliances. Greg developed an important service to reach an important market.

A popular magazine offering many plans for the do-it-yourself market is *Popular Mechanics* magazine. It has between 5 to 7 pages of classified advertisements in each issue—an excellent source to gather mail-order product or service ideas.

The Diet and Health Market

Today's consumer wants not only to eat the right foods but also be healthy enough to keep up an energetic lifestyle. Choose a product or service to help people lose weight, and you might have a winner. For example, many millions of people are walking to stay healthy. These walkers need equipment to help them, such as gauges to measure distance, deterrence devices to help them deal with dogs that might chase them, and proper clothing to be seen on the road at night. Study magazines on walking to help you develop product ideas and sell your product. Remember: Every market will require a line of products or services to reach them.

Mail-Order Owners Market

Some veteran mail-order owners contend you will never get rich in mail order unless you permit others to help you sell your product. Once you get some experience in your own mail-order business you may consider permitting other mail-order owners to buy your product from you. Let them sell it in their sales literature or catalog they send to their customers. This will give you greater exposure to your product or service and will cut down your advertising and handling costs.

Other mail-order owners sell by *drop shipping*. This means advertising a gift product, for instance, a set of beer mugs that sells for $15 plus shipping costs. You advertise this set of mugs in your catalog or sales literature. When you get an order, you send a check for $7.50 plus $1.00 shipping, along with the shipping address of the buyer, to the drop shipper who will ship the product directly to your customer. By using the drop shipping method, you will discover new product ideas and trends in the mail-order field.

PICK YOUR MARKET CAREFULLY

Spend time and effort on your market. Know more about your market than your competition. Many overambitious and overeager mail-order owners try to sell their product without carefully considering their market. Research and pick your market. As you begin to advertise, you will get to know even more about your market and can adjust your advertising and marketing program to reach your objectives. In my mail-order business, I had many customers write to me to ask about my product, and some even called me on the phone to talk about my product. I found that when someone was interested enough to call and inquire about the product, I could explain the product in greater detail, and the customer would buy. The check was in the mail a few days later. When customers respond quickly, you can be sure you have made the match between your product and your target market.

COMMUNICATE WITH YOUR CUSTOMER

Find a way to communicate to your customer. Reach out to your customer like a friend reaches out to another friend. A successful mail-order operation requires happy, satisfied customers. Customers never stay happy unless you make a continuous effort to keep in touch with them. The cow never stays milked; you must milk the cow daily. The customer is your most important challenge. You must keep up a speaking relationship with your customer.

One mail-order owner in New York is always thinking about his customers, and he treats his long-time customers just like family members. He analyzes each order to determine where it came from, the price, and whether a special bonus was offered, and uses this information for future offers. He looks over the inquiries, treats each one as another important message, and answers it promptly to encourage the potential sale. Ask your customer whether he or she is satisfied with your product. Do something to help your customer, and you will do something for yourself.

THE TWO-STEP MAIL-ORDER STRATEGY

Mail order requires a workable strategy to succeed. Back in Chapter 1, the two-step method was discussed as an excellent way for the beginner to start in the business successfully, without a large investment or a lot of risk. The two-step method is when you run a classified advertisement, and then follow up with more information to make the sale.

I recommend this two-step method strongly because I used it to build my mailing list up to 30,000 names. You can do the same if you consider six principles. Below you will find the list of principles, and a brief description of what is required.

1. Select your product or service.
2. Select your target market.
3. Prepare your classified advertisement.
4. Place classified advertisement.
5. Order your products/services.
6. Prepare sales literature.

Principle 1. Choose a product or service you know and enjoy. Review the characteristics of a good mail-order product in Chapter 3.

Principle 2. Select the best possible target market to sell your product. The target market might be teachers, stamp collectors, jewelry buyers, teenagers, or women executives.

Principle 3. Prepare your classified advertisement. The classified advertisement is two or three sentences long, and will be used to call attention to your product or service. Let's say, for instance, your product is a cassette program on "Stress Management for Women Executives." Rather than sell it using a large, expensive display advertisement, you use an inexpensive classified advertisement. Writing classified advertisements will be discussed in Chapter 7.

Principle 4. Place the classified advertisement in a magazine especially geared to your target market. The classified advertisement will ask the reader to send for more information. Review the classified advertisement below.

> Exciting, new stress management cassette program for women executives. Fully guaranteed. Free information: The Executive Company, 800P Melrose St. Goldwest, MO 00001.

The letter ''P'' next to 800 in the address represents a key for the magazine used. The keying method will be discussed in a later chapter. Place more classified advertisements when you find they work for you.

Principle 5. Order enough products or services to handle the orders from your customers. Never advertise until you have products available to service your customers.

Principle 6. Once the potential customer responds to your classified advertisement, you now have the chance to sell him or her completely with your carefully planned sales material. The sales material will include a sales letter filled with all the benefits of your product or service and why they should buy from you. Adding a brochure that shows specific features of your product will add to your selling punch. A reply card summarizes your offer, including price and order information. A reply envelope is enclosed to make it easier to order. (Chapter 9 will cover how to prepare sales material in detail.)

Each magazine has a two- or three-month closing date, which means if you place the advertisement in March, the classified advertisement will not appear until May. This two-month delay gives you an opportunity to prepare the sales literature in time for the appearance of your advertisement. Time management is essential. In Appendix A, I have included a ''Get Started Now'' checklist. Use it as a guide. Set a date for each step and do them one by one.

Why not just mail your sales materials out to get orders in the beginning? There is a basic reason against it: It is too expensive to rent lists and send offers to people you're not sure will buy. It is far better to start off with a small classified advertisement, and then send your full sales literature to people who show interest. I had a student in one of my mail-order seminars who tried to use the direct-mail method in the beginning of his business. He spent thousands of dollars for rental of lists, postage, and printing for his direct-mail package. The direct-mail campaign failed miserably. The student told me that if he had to do it all again he would use the two-step mail-order strategy and build his own house list. Once his house list was built, he could continue his direct mailings to already established customers. I recommend that you wait until your business is clearly established before you attempt the direct-mail method.

Now let's summarize this chapter.

SUMMARY OF KEY POINTS

- Your target market is the most likely customers to purchase your product. It has the desire, money, and interest in your product.

- Keep presenting your product to this target market. Do your homework and get to know your customer completely.
- Your customer goes through various cycles. Learn about the priorities of your customer, and consider these priorities in your business.
- By being sensitive to your customers, you can serve them better.
- The mail-order customer has a bill of rights.
- Give your customer the little extra service to beat your competition.
- The government offers many reports and surveys to help you reach important markets.
- One market may open up other markets for you.
- Business owners are good customers. Career women are buying millions of products and services today. The do-it-yourself market is huge and continues to grow each day.
- Mail-order owners can help you sell some of your products using drop shipping methods.
- Pick your market carefully.
- Communicate in a friendly manner and keep the communication going.
- Your customer needs you and your product; you need your customer.

.

5

Offer Your Customer Your Best

THE *OFFER* IS THE EXACT TERMINOLOGY YOU USE TO DESCRIBE THE PRODUCT, price, terms, bonuses, guarantee, instructions on how to respond, and other important points to your potential mail-order customer. Just as your product must match your customer, your offer must also connect with your potential customer. Your offer must get the order.

YOUR OFFER MUST BE BELIEVABLE

Your offer must get attention, but it must also be believable. When you offer too much product for too little cost your potential customer may turn away. The same applies for too much price for your product. Your customer will be looking for a reasonable price, and something extra to make the purchase worthwhile.

Make your offer attractive by offering a premium, such as a gift or a special book, when your customer spends a certain amount of money. For example, if the customer spends $50 or more, include a free gift with the order.

START YOUR CUSTOMER OFF RIGHT

Try to establish an offer that appeals to your customer. Offer your product as an excellent purchase with good value. For example, a mail-order company in New Jersey offers a yearly desk calendar for $1.98 to introduce their product to the customer. Selling a quality product at a reasonable price ensures customer satisfaction, which will help open the door to future offers and sales. Always give your customer a good lead product and build a relationship from there.

DEVELOP AN OFFER YOUR CUSTOMER WILL UNDERSTAND

Clear communication of the offer is one of the most important mail-order principles discussed in this book. You can choose an excellent product and match it with a clearly defined customer group, but you still must communicate an offer that connects with the customer. The offer must be right for your customer and your product. The essential elements of a successful mail-order offer are shown in Fig. 5-1.

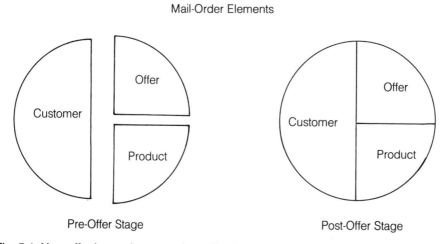

Mail-Order Elements

Pre-Offer Stage   Post-Offer Stage

Fig. 5-1. Your offer is very important in mail order. The offer brings the product idea to the customer to make the sale. The offer will be examined closely before the buying decision is made by the customer. A well-planned offer will open the door to more business for you.

Remember, the offer includes many items including the price, terms, bonuses, and guarantees; each one must be given some consideration based on your customer and your product. Put the pieces together. The following is a list of important points in your offer:

	Your Offer	*Examples*
Product	_____	Instruction booklet
Price	_____	$3.99
Terms	_____	Check/Cash

Bonuses	_____	Free Shipping
Guarantees	_____	Full Guarantee
Instructions	_____	3 Easy Steps
How to Respond	_____	Order Form

Spend some time on each point of your offer. You might want to look at other mail-order offers to determine what elements they include to make their offers attractive. Examine offers of mail-order products outside the field. For example, if you sell gifts you might want to look at offers in the small business field such as office supplies.

Your offer must be well planned. When you develop a good offer it will compete against the best. Put your best effort forward. It will take some time and effort to get it just the way you want, but you must keep in mind that your offer will be closely checked by your customers. If your offer connects with them, you will have a winner. If your offer fails, make the needed adjustments to make it a mail-order winner.

You can use your offer list to write your sales literature or advertisement. You must know what your offer includes so you can express it clearly to others. Many mail-order people spend a great deal of time selecting a product and a market, and spend too little time clearly defining their terms. The offer is the engine car in the mail-order train. Without a strong offer, the whole mail-order program will fail, or slow down with very little success.

GUARANTEES INCREASE SALES

Your offer should include a guarantee to show your customer you will stand behind your product. Some mail-order owners feel that guarantees are costly and might increase the possibility of customers returning the product for a refund. In my experience there are some returns, usually between 3 to 5 percent of the total sales. Some customers are never satisfied; perhaps they expect too much from the product or service. Yet a guarantee will help reach the potential customer who is unsure about buying your product.

Your guarantee means nothing if you take the returned item and fail to refund promptly. Send the money right away so your customer never has anything to complain to others about you and your business practices. When your returns increase to between 10 to 20 percent, give serious consideration about upgrading your product or replacing it with another one. Your guarantee does not cost you; it pays off to have one in your offer.

Make it easy for your customer to respond to you. Your offer must consider the potential customer directly, in order to succeed. For example, a jewelry mail-order owner sells watches and announces new features to his customers. The mail-order offer includes a two-year guarantee, and if the customer is not satisfied, he can return it within two weeks for a full refund. The offer should also allow the customer to use a major credit card to make it easy to purchase. Check with your local bank to find out about accepting credit cards.

INCLUDE AN EXTRA GIFT

Everyone likes something free. Many successful mail-order offers include a free gift as an added incentive to make the sale. Try to blend the free gift with the products or services you offer. For example, a stationery supplies mail-order company in New York offers a small book on letter writing when the customer spends over $25 in his order. A yarn and sewing mail-order company selling sewing kits in Vermont will include free knitting needles when the order is $40 or more. Test your free gift ideas; once you find one that works, continue with it.

POSITIVE OFFERS WORK

Get excited about your product. See it working in your customer's home and think about how your customer will find satisfaction and gain benefits from your product. Some mail-order offers are so positive and exciting, you keep reading the advertisement or sales literature over and over. You keep thinking about how you can get the money together to buy the product.

Other offers fail to excite you enough to reread the offer and take action. A positive offer is essential to your success in mail order. It should include the important features of the product and describe how the customer can benefit—how it will make him or her more attractive or gain more friends. Review the benefits of your product. The positive offer gets the product and customer involved together and makes it easy for the customer to buy. The positive offer will communicate the most key features, such as price or terms, to get the customer.

YOUR PRICE IS IMPORTANT

Make your price as low as possible, but make certain that the price reflects the quality of your product. The price should be fair and give you a reasonable profit. For example, let's say your product is a New England cookbook, filled with century-old recipes. Your cost is $1 for each book. Mail-order prices should be 3 to 4 times your cost. Try to sell the book for $3 to $4 to keep your profits high enough to increase your advertising and promotion.

Many mail-order owners understate their costs. Remember, you must pay for the unit cost of products, postage, advertising, wrapping and shipping costs, inquiries, handling returns, handling bad checks, sales literature, address labels, tape, glue, and other normal business expenses. Even with the office in your home, you do have expenses that must be included in your price.

Accept personal checks from your customers. I have sold thousands of products all over the world and received only one or two returned checks with insufficient funds. My experience has been very positive and I feel certain yours will be positive as well. Most people are honest.

Refer to the Profit/Loss Projection for selling 100 copies of a cookbook. Profit is the difference between the total sales less the expenses incurred to make the sales.

Successful mail-order businesses perform a profit-and-loss projection on each product they sell. When a product fails to sell enough to increase their profits, they consider replacing it with a product to increase their profits and further expand the profits.

Profit/Loss Projection
Able Mail Order Co.
Portland, Maine

Sales (100 copies of book)		$400.00
Expenses		
Product (100 items at $1.00 each)	$100.00	
Transportation In	12.00	
Advertising	25.00	
Sales Literature	10.00	
Office Supplies	5.00	
Shipping Cost (100x39)	39.00	
Total Costs		$191.00
Profit		$209.00

WRITE A CONVINCING OFFER

Writing a convincing advertisement is not an easy task. A winning advertisement is written with conviction and includes important information. Writing a two- or three-sentence offer helps define your mail-order program. Go back to the section entitled ''Develop an Offer Your Customer Will Understand'' on p. 42 and look over your offer points to help you write your offer. The following is a short sample offer.

A unique baby book filled with page after page to record all the essential information on your new baby. Parents and grandparents will enjoy filling this book, page after page. The price is $5.95 plus $1.00 shipping and handling costs. Fully guaranteed. Send your check today.

Write your offer in the space below.

_____

_____

_____

_____

_____

_____

_____

THE OFFER SHOULD BE "YOU" ORIENTED

The successful mail-order owner tries to involve the potential customer with the offer. One way to do this is to use the word "you" as often as possible. For example, the product will make you look more attractive; your friends will respect *you*; *you* will feel more confident; *you* will become the life of the party with this exciting new product. By using the "you" word, you are breaking down any hesitation and showing the customer you can be personal and business-oriented at the same time.

Being personal with your customer adds to your sales. I use a personal letter when I send my sales literature to follow up on my classified advertisement inquiries. In the personal letter, I thank my customers for writing to me and expressed my interest in their success with my newsletter manual. I noticed a sharp increase in sales with the personal letter; my responses increased from around 4 percent to over 15 percent of all inquiries. I recall one customer who included a note to me with his order and stated he had a choice of buying my product or the same product from other companies who offered the same price and the same terms. He told me he decided on my product because of my homespun, personal approach, which was a little different from the competition.

You can print up a printed personal note that looks very much like a handwritten personal note. Some mail-order owners contend that a personal, handwritten note is too time-consuming and costly. Others feel that this is an excellent way to show their customers they will do the little extra service to get the order. A personal note is shown in Fig. 5-2.

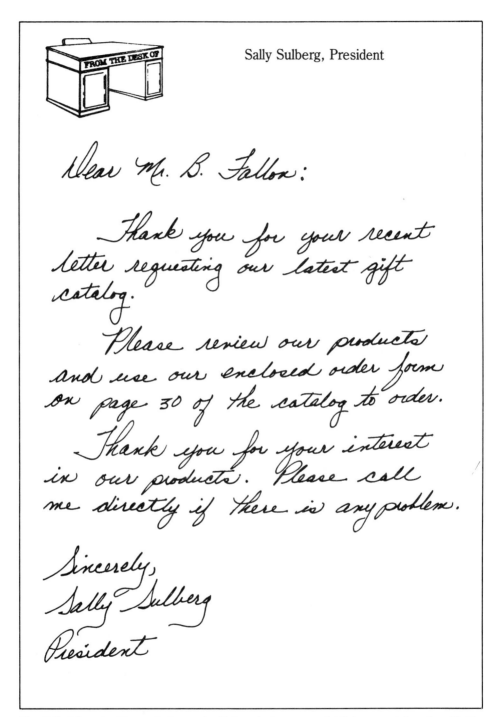

Sally Sulberg, President

Dear Mr. B. Fallon:

Thank you for your recent letter requesting our latest gift catalog.

Please review our products and use our enclosed order form on page 30 of the catalog to order.

Thank you for your interest in our products. Please call me directly if there is any problem.

Sincerely,
Sally Sulberg
President

Fig. 5-2. A handwritten note to a potential customer can establish a special and profitable relationship. Having received the personal attention of the president, the customer is likely to feel your company cares about its customers.

You might want to test the handwritten personal note method when you send sales literature to your customers. To do a test, you could include 25 personal letters for every 50 sales packages you send out. Key the order cards with the letters HWN, for hand-written note on the right-hand corner of the reply card to determine the orders received from personal letter packages. We will spend more time on testing and keying your advertisements in a later chapter.

KNOW YOUR PRODUCT

There is a well-known television commercial about how one investment house makes their money. The commercial points out ''We make money the old fashioned way: We earn it.'' The same rule applies to developing a winning offer; you must earn it by knowing your product completely. How do you find out about all the features, benefits, advantages, and disadvantages of your product? By using your product, by taking it apart, by asking other people about it, and by getting involved with the product or service. For example, I worked in a large Boston advertising agency, and the advertising writer for a large bank wrote advertisements about various savings accounts offered by the bank. In order to get closer to the customer, the writer went to the bank and opened an account of his own to get more information about the account. The writer learned some important facts about the savings account.

Nothing is better than personal experience with a product to write about it in an exciting and realistic manner. To make an offer on fishing equipment, try out the fishing equipment on your next fishing trip. Determine what the most exciting and identifiable benefit or advantage your product offers over other products is. Use it, touch it, feel it, throw it in the air, smell it, search for the uniqueness of your product or service before you make your offer. When your customer has plenty of information about the product, he or she can make the buying decision.

YOUR TERMS COUNT

Your product is excellent, your price fair. Now you must have favorable terms. Your terms are how you will accept payment, and how and when you will ship the product to your customer. Many mail-order owners include the shipping free-of-charge to make the offer more attractive. Another mail-order company from California that sells gifts by mail offers a choice of one of three free gifts when the order totals $25 or more. The gifts include an all-purpose wrench, a set of trinket boxes, and a handy flashlight.

Some mail-order owners accept charge cards to make their offer more attractive and speed up the orders. When you accept charge cards there will be additional charges to you by your bank. You might want to start your business without the charge cards, and then add them to your offer when the business is more established. For more information on the charge cards, check with the manager of your bank.

EXAMINE OTHER OFFERS

Look for other offers in magazines, newspapers, and direct-mail offers. Which offers make you read them over again and again? Why did these offers appeal to you? What do you look for in an offer to make you buy the product or service? One question I like to ask during my mail-order seminars is ''How many people purchased a product or service by mail during the last six months?'' Usually, at least half the students raise their hands. I then ask them why they purchased the product or service. Examining your own decision-making process when making a mail-order purchase will help you construct your own offer. For example, some customers will look at price first as one of the most important factors in the offer. Other customers are primarily concerned about the quality of the product or service and will not respond unless the quality is the highest level possible. Joe Sugarman, a leading mail-order owner mentioned earlier in the book, offers many details about his products, carefully showing benefit after benefit, so his customers are aware of the complete details on the product. His customers respond by buying products and services in large quantities.

MOTIVATE YOUR CUSTOMER TO ORDER

Succeeding in the mail-order business requires salesmanship and an understanding of what motivates your customer to purchase your product or service. Human motivation is defined as a mental force that induces an act. Motivation in mail order is the process of moving the customer from the mental stage, when they are just thinking about the product, to the physical stage, when they actually fill out your order card and send you that check for your product.

As you develop your offer, remember your customer has more on his or her mind than purchasing your AM/FM portable clock radio. Your customer also has to deal with the electric bill, telephone bill, grocery bill, rent payment, mortgage payment, insurance payment, and many other bills. You are competing with entertainment suppliers and the bank as well. Your customer must decide whether he or she would rather spend money on your clock radio or on a night on the town. The customer may also compare the product with the option of putting the money into his or her savings account. The competition is intense, not only with other mail-order companies offering products or services, but with other obligations and opportunities offered to your customer. Your offer must motivate the customer to buy your product.

A FREE TRIAL OFFER

Everyone wants a good bargain. Why not include a special offer and permit your customer to try the product or service before they buy it? This practice is frequently used in the information services business, whereby they will send you a copy of the newsletter for one or two months, and you can decide whether or not you want to continue with the service. The advantage to the customer is the opportunity to try your product or service with no obligation to pay for it unless he or she agrees to accept it. The advantage to you, the seller, is the opportunity to get more people to try your product; if your quality is high, there will be additional sales. The disadvantage to you is you get more customers who might just want to try your product, without a real interest or motivation to buy your product.

To get the orders before the Christmas deadline, a mail-order company in Minneapolis offers a free trial offer and free shipping and handling charges when the customer orders before December 16th. This company sells close-out merchandise, including luggage, housewares, tools, and electronic products. The objective of their offer is to get the customer to try their product once, and then send the customer catalog after catalog to keep the customer buying. The offer must excite the customer enough to try your product or service. Nothing happens until the customer buys your product. You are selling yourself when you try to sell to your customer in the offer. Get excited about your product and the value it represents, and sell, sell, sell.

THE OFFER UNDERSTANDS THE VALUE OF A CUSTOMER

A customer is an unknown to you. The customer may buy one product from you or buy hundreds of products from you. Some customers will buy for a few years and then stop. The greatest challenge for you will be to keep your customers buying month-after-month, year-after-year. I had one customer from Canada who purchased every product in my catalog. I was really excited to receive the order; it meant my offer impressed the customer enough to make such a large order. Set a goal to make your offer so attractive people will buy all your products.

SUMMARY OF KEY POINTS

- Your offer is the most important element in your mail-order program. It must be believable, or it will fail.
- Make your product appeal to your customer.
- When you value your product or service, it will be reflected in your offer.
- Develop a message your customer can understand.

- Make a list of all the items that make up your offer.
- Consider your customer's needs and make it easy to order from you.
- Consider including an extra gift.
- Positive offers work.
- Choose a price that is profitable and attractive to your customer.
- Do a profit/loss projection before you develop your offer.
- Make the offer personal to the customer. Some mail-order companies include personal handwritten notes to increase the orders.
- A winning offer will require some time and effort.
- Look at other mail-order offers in advertisements, catalogs, and sales literature.
- Consider a free trial offer to get your customer to consider your product or service more seriously.
- Your offer must understand the value of a customer; give him or her the best offer possible.

6

Write the Words that Sell

I WORKED FOR A LARGE ADVERTISING AGENCY IN BOSTON SHORTLY AFTER I graduated from college. It was a rewarding experience working with artists and writers to develop advertisements for various products. Advertising agencies plan, develop, and produce advertising and services for others. I recall the day the president asked one of the writers to make a trip to New York to receive an advertising award for an award-winning advertisement for our client, a national golf equipment manufacturer. The advertisement won the award because it informed and persuaded the customer to take action; it had a clear purpose. When the advertisement is well planned, clearly informs the customer, and directs the customer to buy, it will be a winner for you.

KNOW YOUR AUDIENCE

As mentioned in Chapter 4, you must know and understand your market, or audience, in order to reach them. You will be writing to golf players, watch buyers, gift buyers, farmers, electricians, secretaries, veterans, widows, homeowners, business owners, accountants, or health food buyers. Keep the audience in mind; pay sharp attention to their age, background, interests, needs, and future needs. Keep your relationship in mind in your writing. For example, if you sell gifts, make certain you write clearly about the differences between your products and the competitors'. Tell your customer how you researched many gifts so you can offer them the best gifts available today. Talk to your customer like he or she is your best friend.

GET EXCITED ABOUT YOUR PRODUCT OR SERVICE

You will move your customers to act on your offer if you show them you are fired up about it. Consider the special features of your product; give examples of how the product can help your customer. Express yourself fully. Put your personality into the advertisement or sales literature. Tell your customer why you picked this product or service from others. For example, let's say your product is a manual on how to get a job. Describe all the important steps necessary to attain the job, and give the reasons why this manual is the best one on the market today. Your customer will pick up on your enthusiasm and buy from you.

YOUR PROPOSAL MUST ANSWER QUESTIONS CLEARLY

A confused customer wrote back to a mail-order company and wanted an explanation of just what the company was trying to sell. This is a signal that the sales letter did not communicate the product or service clearly enough. What are you selling? Answer that question before you move ahead with your proposal. You are proud of your product, so why not take the necessary time to explain it fully? The customer is also asking why he should buy the product. Answer this question by fully describing the product, including features, benefits, advantages, and any other special terms you offer, such as a money-back guarantee. Turn the customer around with copy to convince him or her you have a product with excellent value.

GET ATTENTION

Your potential customer is tired. He has just returned home from work, and, with his feet propped up on the stool, is reading your sales letter or your advertisement in the magazine. Hit him on the head to get his attention. A strong headline will do this for you. Pull him away from the television set so that he can finish reading your offer. Attention is attained or lost in the first few seconds. When your potential customer is hooked on your first few phrases or sentences in your proposal, he will continue reading. Now you have cultivated interest.

WRITE A COMMANDING HEADLINE

Your reader is deluged with hundreds of advertisements and messages during the average day. Your challenge is to stop the reader and appeal to him to start reading your message, with the hope he will continue to read and then respond with an order. Show your reader you have some breakthrough ideas. Let's look at some possible headlines for a food blender you plan to sell by mail.

1. Free 10-day trial reservation
2. How to save time and money with latest food blender
3. A food blender that does what you want
4. Your own versatile kitchen helper
5. 25 breakthrough ways to serve delightful meals
6. A food preparation idea of the decade
7. Full factory warranty and 21st-century design

Make a list of as many headlines as possible for your product or service. Some will be sharp and clear, others will be awkward. Read them over and choose the best one to start your mail-order proposal.

INTEREST OPENS THE DOOR

Your customer is showing interest by continuing to read your proposal. The door is now open. Just like a door-to-door salesperson, you must keep talking to keep the customer interested. Tell your customer about the key features of your product. Tell your customer how other people have enjoyed the product in the past. Tell the customer how you will stand behind the product with a full money-back guarantee. Now you have cultivated desire.

DESIRE PERMITS YOU TO EXPAND YOUR PROPOSAL

Once you have gained attention and interest, you not only have the customer's front door opened, you are now able to sit down together and discuss the product or service. As you write, you will think of more and more selling points and important features. Money- and time-saving features can be added in now. The customer is now in the buying mood.

REQUEST ACTION

Perhaps the most important part of the writing process is when you ask for the order. Tell the customers how they can order. Tell them to send a check for $9.99 and to fill out the enclosed order card and return it in the enclosed envelope. Too often mail-order owners fail to ask for action in the order and never receive it. You cannot get the order unless you ask for it.

PUTTING THE PIECES TOGETHER

The AIDA (Attention, Interest, Desire, Action) approach to writing successful mail-order advertisements is very popular. To outline this approach, let's review each part of the formula with a writing example.

ATTENTION   Headline: "You're a Special Person"

INTEREST   Why? Because you responded to my classified adver-
                  tisement for more information on how to start a home busi-
                  ness. You have a special dream and you're willing to take
                  the necessary steps to make your dream come true.
                      Millions of people start home businesses, and my new
                  manual "How to Start a Home Business" is filled with
                  hundreds of new ideas, techniques, and strategies to help
                  you start your own.
                      This book will help you turn that spare room into your
                  own business—in your spare time, even while you continue
                  with your present job.

DESIRE   You will be your own boss. You will set your own
                  hours. You will save money because your commute to work
                  will be about five minutes—the time it takes to walk to your
                  spare room or basement. You will be able to do the work
                  you want to do, rather than the work your boss picks out
                  for you. By starting your own business, you will be your
                  own person.

ACTION   Now make your dream come true. Fill out the enclosed
                  reply card and write your check for $14.95 for this exciting
                  book. Act today and watch your opportunities grow tomor-
                  row.

Let your copy flow in a logical order. Make it easy for the reader to act on
your proposal. Build the proposal in such a manner that the reader cannot resist
trying your product. Check your writing to make certain there are enough reasons to buy your product or service. Your proposal should look beneficial and
worthwhile.

INTERESTING WRITING WORKS

When you meet someone for the first time, you try to say worthwhile things to
make a good impression. Successful mail-order copy is interesting because it
shows the product or service in a unique or different manner. It might show the
new features; it might detail the most important benefits; it might even challenge
the reader to find a better product at a better price. Interesting copy informs the
reader how the product or service can become a part of his or her life. For example, if you want to sell an electric food blender, why not tell the reader how he or
she can now blend, chop, mince, grate, slice, and shred food in minutes? This
product can save the reader precious time and money. Find a theme and build on
it.

USE A THEME

Good writing follows a theme so the reader can relate and remember your proposal. For example, in a fishing tackle ad, the theme might be to show the uniqueness and quality of the products. If you are selling a book on New England recipes you could use the theme of using New England's seafood and fish specialities. Your theme broadens your advertisement and gives your reader a better understanding of your product or service. It permits your reader to use your product in his or her life.

WRITING IS A PROCESS

Writing is very difficult work. Good writing requires time, effort, and an understanding of the process. Your first advertisement or sales letter may not please you. Revise it. Cut out the excessive words. Take out that phrase that is confusing to you. Put the writing away for a day and read it over as the potential customer would read it. Good writing, like good food, requires time and effort. I have a friend who attended a fine-art school and is an artist specializing in oil painting of seascapes. When he first started in the art field, he purchased a sketchbook, and each day he would make a sketch, perhaps of a bike, horse, dog, or a chair. This sketchbook is filled with many drawings—some good, some fair, and some poor. The sketchbook served as a way for my friend to increase his confidence and his skill at the same time.

Writing, like art, is a process. Keep trying until you get your advertisement or sales letter just the way you want it.

TESTING COPY

Some mail-order companies write two different sales letters to sell their product. One sales letter might focus on the gift appeal to your product; the other sales letter might focus on the price and durability of your product. One letter might be directed at the man in the family; the other letter at the woman. Successful mail-order companies continue to test and test. Suppose a company receives 100 inquiries from their classified or display advertisement. They might send sales letter A to 50 inquiries and letter B to the remaining inquiries. The reply card will be marked with an A or B to designate the sales letter used. When you find that sales letter A is selling better than sales letter B, you can then use it until sales begin to drop.

TELL YOUR READER ABOUT YOURSELF

I have a good friend who works for a large personal-care retailer. The company is successful because it offers good-quality products, convenience, price, selection, and cleanliness to their customers. Since you cannot expect a customer to come to you, your copy must communicate the special features of your company. Do you expect to send the product out immediately after the order is placed? Tell the reader about this special service. Do you guarantee your product fully? Are you willing to give your customers their money back if your product is not fully accepted? Tell them about it in your advertisement or sales literature. Be confident about yourself and your product or service. Tell your readers how important they are to you. Inform your readers about your willingness to work hard to get their business, and even harder to continue doing business in the future. Tell your readers why you went into the mail-order business, and give reasons why they should buy from you. Find out what the competition is failing to do, and then deliver it to stand out from the crowd.

MAKE CLAIMS AND BACK THEM UP

Good mail-order copy gives facts, figures, benefits, advantages, and features that make you more attractive to your reader. Go beyond the claim by stating the proof the reader will need before purchasing your product. For example, if you state your blender can do many things, enumerate them for the reader. If you guarantee the blade in your blender, inform the reader of the guarantee. Remember, the reader does not know you. You live in Albany, New York, she lives in Elmwood, Illinois, thousands of miles away. Make your claim, but give the backup as well. Give testimonials to the reader. What reactions do you get from your customers about your product? Keep the letters from satisfied customers, who enjoyed your product or service. Write back and thank them for their letters, and ask for their permission to use their letters in future advertisements or sales letters and catalogs in the future. Nothing sells better than good testimonials from satisfied customers.

GOOD COPY SELLS

Good copy is similar to the delightful aroma of fresh coffee first thing in the morning. It creates a visual image in your mind. It is the sizzle of the steak grilling in your kitchen. Good copy helps your reader visualize your product in his or her own home and takes the reader on a journey from the mental state of simply thinking about the product, to the physical state when the reader is ready to take out the checkbook from the desk drawer to buy your product.

Good copy, like good food, takes time, preparation, and revision after revision to get it right. Once your copy is right, the reader will grade it by speaking to you, not in words, but by action. The reader will buy your product. That is the most important goal in mail order: to present the product in such a convincing way, the reader will buy it.

AVOID SMUGNESS

Some mail-order companies become too confident after some initial success and lose their relationship with their reader. The reader must be reminded time and time again of why you are the best, where you come from, and what you sell. The reader is a busy person and cannot remember everything. Make statements so the reader can remember you and your product better. Be willing to stand up for the basics.

Good copy avoids smugness, it offers straightforward words that inspire and motivate the reader to act.

LEAVE GOOD COPY ALONE

Once you get your copy just the way you want it, leave it alone. Let it do the work. Send it on its way to the readers of the world. When the orders start coming in a steady stream, permit the copy to do the work for you. Don't touch anything until the orders slow up. Why fix it when it isn't broken? Too often mail-order owners keep changing their copy and get mixed results. Work on your copy to get it right, then test it, then analyze the results from your first few advertisements. Did you make a profit from the advertisement?*

Many successful mail-order owners believe you must advertise in mail order or stay out completely. Keep advertising to keep your product in front of your customers.

All successful companies sell something the customer is buying. This sounds very simple, but too often the mail-order seller simply assumes the customer knows the product or service and will buy it without being convinced that the product is the one for him. Use all the information about your customer you discovered from Chapter 2 and 3, in your copy. Your copy must sell your product. Keep that in mind at all times.

HIRING OTHERS TO WRITE YOUR COPY

I recommend that you write your own copy, because you will gain valuable experience and you know the product or service better than anyone else. Some people feel their writing skills are not strong enough. In this case you can turn the writing over to a professional advertising writer—someone who will perform the writing for a fee. The writer should have mail-order advertising writing experience that includes advertisements, sales letters, and brochures for the mail-order market. You can find some writers in the business section of your

---

* A profit is the difference between the amount of money you received in orders, let's say $400.00, less the cost of the advertisement, $60.00, the cost of your products, $150.00, the cost of your shipping and handling costs, $30.00, which equals a profit of $160.00. Use the $160.00 for your next two or three advertisements.

telephone book. Ask the writer if he or she has mail-order experience. Ask about seeing samples of their past work and about their rates. Get a written estimate of their rates before you agree to hire the writer. Pay for the job only after you see the final product.

When you receive the sales letter, brochure, or ad, read the copy completely. Does it communicate to the reader? Does it show the product or service in the best possible light? Does it follow the AIDA formula? Does it ask for the order? Would you order the product or service if you read the copy? If the answer is yes to all of these questions, there is a good possibility the copy will do the job. If there is something in the letter that is weak, or you would like corrected, let the writer know about it. You are the customer, and before you pay for the letter or writing project, make certain you are completely satisfied.

WHAT ARE THE RATES FOR A PROFESSIONAL WRITER?

Rates vary from writer to writer, and from one geographical area to another. For example, a mail-order owner in Maine paid $400 for copy on a two-page brochure, a reply card, and an envelope. The normal prices are simple estimates. You might pay more or less for the writing.

Estimates for Writing Fees

- *Sales Letter*—$150 to $400 for one or two pages.
- *Direct Mail Packages*—$1,000 and up including sales letter, reply card, and envelope. Price depends upon writer's mail-order writing skills, experience, and reputation.
- *Direct Mail Catalog*—$10 to $50 per page, depending upon the size of the catalog. The longer the catalog, the smaller the price per page.

Remember, these rates are only estimates. Choose the best copy possible, and choose a rate that you can afford. A winning sales letter will bring in many orders and you can use it over and over again, until the profits decrease and you need a change in your copy.

CHOOSE THE GRAPHICS TO COMPLEMENT YOUR COPY

A picture is worth a thousand words. In mail-order selling nothing sells like a good photograph or illustration of your product, especially showing the product in action. See Fig. 6-1. If you are selling a food blender, a good photograph showing the product in use will help increase your sales. Use a photograph with detailed copy to highlight your product or service. By using copy and illustrations together, communicate your message to the reader.

You might also want to use clip art to add a graphic element to your sales material. Clip art is copyright-free artwork, that can be cut out and photostatted.

CAREER SUCCESS ON VIDEO

Career success means knowledge. Knowledge of yourself, and the skills necessary to manage others. A new video is available to help you set your goals, build teamwork, use better time management, get more accomplished, build positive communication skills and many more.

Your supervision classroom is at work, home or anyplace where you have access to a VCR. Save time and money, by making an investment in your own career success (36 minutes; VHS only). For more information write to: Executive Mail Order Co., 100A Glenview Rd. Winchester, MA 00001

Fig. 6-1. This display advertisement uses a drawing to show the video in use. It identifies the product. Notice how the mail-order company uses the two step method to gather responses before the full sales literature is sent out.

Clip art can be used to illustrate your product or as borders or decorative motifs. Check with your local bookstore to see what clip art designs are available in your area.

CHECKING YOUR COPY IS CRUCIAL

Read over your letter, brochure, or advertisement to see whether or not it is ready to go out into the world of difficult to sell readers. Go down the following list and check yes or no on each statement. Recheck your copy for each statement in which you answered no to correct it.

Mail-Order Copy Checklist for Success

Yes	No	
—	—	1. Do you have a central idea?
—	—	2. Do you describe your product or service clearly?
—	—	3. Is it believable?
—	—	4. Do you show how your product is different?
—	—	5. Have you used the AIDA formula?
—	—	6. Do you ask for your order?
—	—	7. Do you tell them how to take action?
—	—	8. Would you order the product or service after reading this copy?
—	—	9. Is it exciting enough to get the order for you?

SUMMARY OF KEY POINTS

- Your words tell your story. Make your words work hard for you.
- Use words that sell. Your words must excite the over-busy, deluged reader to act.
- You must know your audience.
- Get excited about your product or service.
- State your proposal clearly. When you have trouble making yourself clear, the reader will stop reading and put your sales letter in his wastebasket.
- Knock on the reader's door with an attention-grabbing headline. Open the reader's door with interesting copy.
- Expand your copy to create desire for your reader.
- Ask the reader to act.
- Put all the AIDA pieces together.
- Interesting writing connects to readers.
- Use a theme to help the reader remember your message.
- Test your copy.
- Put yourself into the copy.
- Make claims carefully and then prove them.
- Avoid smugness, reach out to your reader.
- Once the copy is written, leave it alone.
- Professional writers can produce quality copy work.
- Choose graphics that help you show your product most effectively.
- Review the copy checklist before you approve your final copy.

7

Winning Classified
Advertisements

CLASSIFIED ADVERTISEMENTS ARE SMALL-SPACE ADS THAT ATTRACT READERS to respond to your offer. The classified advertisements are an excellent way to sell using the two-step method, whereby the reader sends for more information, and you follow up with the full sales package.

Classified advertisements are easy to write because they are usually only two or three sentences long. However, the competition is stiff; many other mail-order owners are also trying to get the readers to respond to them.

Classified advertisements are sold by the word. For example, if your advertisement is 20 words long, and the cost is $4 per word, the total price will be $80.

A CASE HISTORY

In all my seminars dealing with mail order, I like to offer this case history of using classified advertising to build up your customer list. A number of years ago I developed a manual that offered advice on how to start a newsletter. I placed my own classified advertisement in a business-opportunity magazine called *Free Enterprise Magazine*; the magazine is now out of business. I received 80 responses from this advertisement, as well as a few orders. This got me started in the field, and I continued to place advertisements in national magazines over and over again. Within five years I built my list up to over 30,000 names of people that responded to me or purchased products from me.

Notice how classified advertising led to the direct-mail method of operation. Now I can mail out 2,500 names each month of the year without duplication of names. I can send these names different offers each month. I can rent these names out to other people in the mail-order business, only because I was successful in my classified advertising program.

CLASSIFIED ADVERTISEMENTS IN MAGAZINES

What magazines are best for classified advertising? Many magazines have a large classified advertising section. Magazine publishers earn profits with these classified sections, give their readers an extra service, and want the advertisers to be successful selling their products.

Look over and carefully examine the magazines that have a classified advertising section. What kinds of products are they trying to sell? How long have these classified advertisements appeared? One month? Three months? Six months? One year? Two years? You can be sure that if the advertisement is listed for at least one year straight, the advertisement is paying off for the advertiser. In a recent seminar, one gentleman asked about how to select the best magazine or magazines for advertising. My answer was simple: Test and research into the field. Try different magazines to determine the best pull for your orders. Also read back issues of magazines to determine who is advertising over and over.

When you find a product that is advertised by classified advertising for month after month, it must be paying off for the advertiser. By reviewing the magazines you get an opportunity to see the various products and services sold by classified advertisements. One of the most popular magazines for the advertising of classified advertising is *Popular Mechanics* magazine. Each month this excellent magazine has six or eight pages filled with classified advertisements. Another magazine that has a large classified advertising section is *Popular Science* magazine. Both of these magazines advertise many different products. Some of the categories include books and periodicals, cameras and photo supplies, hobbies and collections, sporting goods, jokes and novelties, stamp collecting, coins and currency, musical instruments, profitable occupations, money-making opportunities, sign painting and cartooning, winemaking, and many, many more. Which category would be the best one for your product? What categories have advertisers with products similar to yours? Find the very best category for your advertisement. You need the proper category to sell your product.

HOW DO YOU WRITE YOUR CLASSIFIED AD?

The most important point in your classified advertisement is that you get the most important message to your potential customers. Tell them about your product. Tell them how the product will benefit them. Take a sheet of paper and list all the benefits and uses of your product. Be sure you write down every one. Now that you have listed them, choose the most important benefits and uses of your product.

Now write a classified advertisement for your product. You can get some ideas from the classified advertisements in other magazines. *Never* copy an advertisement, for this is against the law. However, you can get *ideas* from other advertisements. When you write the advertisement, make sure you include the most important uses of your product and the benefits the user will get from your product. When you get your advertisement written, read it over a few times and see that it gets the proper message across to the customers. Once you determine that your advertisement gets the message across you can delete any extra words. Use only the words that are necessary to get action.

Once you create an advertisement that works, you should continue to use it until it stops pulling for you. You will find you will use the winning classified over and over again.

Make your advertisement easy to read. Use simple words in your advertisement so that people understand your message and can take action. Every word in your classified advertisement must be a winner and every word must be factual. All the words must work together to tell and sell your product or story. An advertisement that is just a fair advertisement will not do the job for you. You want a *profitable* advertisement and profitable advertisements are not written in five or ten minutes. It takes a long time to put the profitable advertisement together, but once the advertisement is completed, you are on your way to success. Refer to the list below for the rules for successful classified advertising.

Rules for Successful Classified Advertising

- Write your offer in all of its details before you edit it to make your classified ad.
- Do have your literature ready when your ad appears. It's a mistake to delay an answer to any inquiry.
- Follow the rule of good advertising in your classifieds, Attention, Interest, Desire, and Action. Use the AIDA principle discussed in an earlier chapter.
- List your name or company name with each advertisement. It will cut your returns if prospects reply to just a street or post office box address.
- Don't attempt to sell an item over $3.00 directly from a classified ad. You can offer something at a greater price, but then invite inquiries to receive your literature to close the sale.
- Try to qualify prospects for very specialized information by offering literature that informs, as well as sells – and make a charge for it.

- Offer a money-back guarantee when you request money in your classified advertisement.
- Do advertise consistently. Many people will respond only after they have seen your ad for awhile and become familiar with your name.
- Do be truthful in all your advertising claims.

While constructing your classified advertisement, be careful not to make claims about your product that are untrue. People will never buy your product again if they are unsatisfied with it. You can build a good list of qualified and satisfied customers if you are truthful in your advertising and sell quality products. People know quality when they see it. People will not be fooled by untruthful advertising and poor-quality products. To sell a line of your products you must convince them to buy your first product.

Before you place your classified advertisement into a magazine, look it over carefully. Does it look like a profitable advertisement? Is it worded carefully? Do you make all your words count? Did you make it easy for the potential customers to take advantage of your offer? Will the prospective customers know what action to take to get to your product? You may even consider permitting an experienced mail-order or advertising person to look it over for you.

SELECTING A MAGAZINE

Try to select a magazine that is noted for its classified advertising section. Choose a magazine that has millions of readers. This will give you a better chance to sell your product. Don't be misled by inexpensive classified rates for some magazines—sometimes the inexpensive rate is a signal that the magazine has fewer subscribers. Spend the money on a good magazine with a good circulation and you will get better results. Figure 7-1 shows how easy it is to place a classified advertisement. Figure 7-2 is an example of classified advertisements.

ADVERTISE REGULARLY

Don't make the mistake many people in the mail-order business make. They write one classified advertisement and place it into one magazine. When they get poor or average results from that one advertisement, they immediately quit advertising. You cannot build a mail-order business on one advertisement. Successful classified advertisers must advertise on a continual basis to get the best results. Remember, no one knew about your product or your company before you put that ad into the magazine. Remember how I built my list to 30,000 by advertising regularly?

People do not always buy your product the first time they see your advertisement in the magazine. They may want your product, but many people are

Classified Advertising Order Form

1507 Dana Avenue ● Cincinnati, Ohio 45207 ● 513-531-2222/800-234-0963/FAX 513-531-4744

Rates effective with January 1990 issue

Date of order _____

Classified Display
Small display ads (cuts, headlines, illustrations, rules etc.) of 1-3 inches in depth and 2¼ inches wide. There is also a one-time charge of $10 per inch for typesetting if needed. Contact your representative for rates for larger sizes.

	1 issue	3 issues*	6 issues*	12 issues*
per inch/per issue	$170	$155	$145	$125

Reading Notices (Non-Commissionable)
15 word minimum. All reading notices must be prepaid. Box number service is $20 per month. Street number, street, city, state and zip code count as four words. Area code and phone number count as two words.

	1 issue	3 issues*	6 issues*	12 issues*
per word/per issue	$3.75	$3.00	$2.40	$2.10

*During a contract year of 12 consecutive issues.

Name _____   _____

Address _____
(Include your home address for our records if you are using a box number in your ad.)

City _____ State _____ Zip _____

Phone _____
(Where you can be reached during regular business hours.)

Authorizing Signature _____

☐ Reading Notice: _____ Words

☐ Classified Display: _____ Inches

Classification _____ Issue(s) _____

Copy _____

_____

_____

_____

_____

Note: All the above information must be completed or the ad will not be processed.

See Other Side For a List of Publisher's Standard Classifications, Closing Dates and Other Important Information.

Fig. 7-1. Magazines make it easy for you to place your classified advertisement by including an advertising order form. It takes just a few minutes to complete on your typewriter or by hand. Some magazines include the classified order form in the magazine. (Continued.)

Contract And Copy Regulations

1. Payment in full must accompany order.
2. A sample of the product and/or promotional material must accompany initial orders.
3. Advertisers offering literary services must send a resume of their experience, along with a sample critique. Agents must submit a 12-month list of sales.
4. Reading notices are set, at the publisher's discretion, with the first few words in bold face type.
5. Key numbers are not guaranteed, nor is any other type set by the publisher.
6. The publisher reserves the right to refuse any ad for any reason with or without notice.
7. Classification heading requests are subject to the publisher's approval. A special classification will be charged $30.
8. Recognized advertising agencies are permitted 15% commission on Classified/Display ads only when submitting camera ready copy.
9. Proofs for Classified/Display ads are available upon request.

Standard Classification Headings

Books/Pamphlets
Business Opportunities
Cartooning
Collaborators
Comedy Writing
Computer Software
Conferences
Contests
Contest Promotions
Critiquing
Editing/Revising
Education, Instruction
Gifts
Grants/Fellowships
Health
Help Wanted
Illustrators
Literary Agents
Literary Services
Mail Order Merchandise
Manuscripts Wanted
Miscellaneous
Personals
Photography
Poetry
Printing/Typesetting
Real Estate
Research
Scriptwriting
Self-Publishing
Songwriting
Stationery/Supplies
Subsidy Publishing
Tapes
Vacations
Writer's Tools
Writers Wanted

Issuance and Ad Closing Dates for 1990

Issue	Ad Closing	On Sale
January	October 17	December 12
February	November 21	January 11
March	December 19	February 13
April	January 16	March 13
May	February 20	April 10
June	March 20	May 10
July	April 17	June 12
August	May 15	July 12
September	June 19	August 9
October	July 17	September 11
November	August 21	October 11
December	September 18	November 13

All orders must be received in our office by the closing date for the issue requested.

PAYMENT by Visa/MasterCard accepted with advertising orders of three or more consecutive issues.

☐ Visa
☐ MasterCard   # _____

Expiration Date   Month _____ Year _____

Amount $ _____

Signature _____

Fig. 7-1. Continued. Second page of a typical classified order form.

Earn money writing newsletters. Free report. Eagle Mail Order Company. 15 Main Street, Anytown, Massachusetts 00091

Exciting, new, safe children's toys. Free catalog. Betty's Toy Company, 11M Monroe Street, Newark, NJ 00001

New furniture—50% off. Two hundred major companies. Free brochure. Smith House, 1100A Noone Street, Winchester, NH 00002

Personal notecards and art prints. Free no obligation catalog. Williams Art Studio, 889D E. 5th, Seattle, WA 00003

Fig. 7-2. People enjoy purchasing new, exciting products and services. Your classified advertisement starts the buying process. Notice all three advertisements include a key next to the street number to determine which magazine accounted for the response.

lazy and don't take action on your product the first time. If you advertise the next month, the people that wanted your product the previous month will be reminded of your product and many will buy. When people see your advertisement in the magazine more than once, they feel that your company is substantial and not a quick money-making enterprise. Now they are in a better frame of mind to do business with you.

Don't get discouraged on the results of your first or second advertisement. You must continue to advertise and test your advertisement. You must continue to try new advertisements even if after two or three months you are not successful in your advertising.

What do most advertisements in classified sections attempt to do? Most of the classified advertisements try to get the prospective customers to write for more details about the product or service. When they write to you for details you can send them complete information. Now you can do a complete selling job. You can send out your sales letter, a brochure or circular, and an order card. The prospective customer can read fully about your product and make a decision.

You want to get as large a percentage of sales out of the inquiries as possible. Some mail-order businesses get as much as 5 percent or 10 percent of the people they send information to. When you send your information out to the people who make the inquiries, make sure that your literature is professionally printed on good-looking stationery. We will discuss this more fully in a later chapter. Prospective customers will judge you and your product by the ''look'' of your sales literature. If it is printed well, and your literature is written clearly, convincingly, and honestly, you will receive the orders for your product.

SUMMARY OF KEY POINTS

- Classified advertisements are an inexpensive way to sell to your target market.

- Read other classified advertisements, and then write a winning classified advertisement to highlight your product or service.

- Classified advertisements can build your house list.

- Take the necessary time to write your classified ad correctly.

- Select the best magazine possible to make it work. Magazines that offer more than 4 pages of classified advertisements will give you a better chance for success.

- Trying to sell your product right from the classified advertisement is very difficult. Most customers want more information before they send their money. Follow up with your sales package.

8

Choosing the Best Magazine Advertising

THE PROPER SELECTION OF THE BEST POSSIBLE MAGAZINES IN WHICH TO ADVER-
tise is an important part of your mail-order business. Choose the right magazine
to attract the best possible customer—especially customers with the money and
the desire for your product or service. Magazines segment the target market for
you. For example, people interested in building and fixing mechanical things read
a magazine like *Popular Mechanics*, sports fans read *Sports Illustrated*, people
interested in starting a small business will read *Business Opportunities* to keep
up with the latest information.

The most important advantage to magazine advertising is the length of life of
a magazine. It will stay around the house two or three months, perhaps as long
as six months to one year. Some readers of magazines keep the magazines for
many years before they throw them out. This long life will help you increase your
orders and inquiries. Orders and letters of interest will continue to appear in
your mailbox many months after the advertisement appeared.

KNOW THE CIRCULATION OF THE MAGAZINE

The total number of copies sold by a magazine is the *circulation*. Circulation figures are reported in each magazine company's Audit Bureau of Circulation Statements. A magazine company will publish their circulation once yearly in their

magazine. The circulation of a magazine is comprised of subscribers and readers. Subscribers are those who are willing to spend their hard-earned money to read the magazine. When you purchase an advertisement from the magazine company, you're really purchasing the right to offer your message to the subscribers. Some magazines send free magazines to readers; paid subscribers are more important to you.

"Readers," also called the *pass-along circulation* are the total amount of people reading the magazine. Readers include the members of the subscriber's family, people in the waiting room of the doctor's office, people in the office that read the subscriber's copy, and so forth. There are usually 3 to 4 readers to each subscriber. Subscribers buy the magazine, will read the magazine with more interest, and are more apt to order from you. The magazine might state they offer 50,000 subscribers and 200,000 readers, so only 50,000 people are paying for the magazine to be delivered to their home or business.

REVIEW MAGAZINES YOURSELF

The best way to select the best possible magazine is to review the magazines yourself. Look over the products and services in these magazines. What type of products are advertised? What type of articles are included? Do they have business articles, career articles, home improvement or gardening articles that are interesting and will keep the subscriber busy reading long enough so that they will spot your ad? Does the magazine have a classified advertisement section? How long is it? A small classified advertisement section indicates a poor response for the advertisers and should be avoided until the section increases in size. *Popular Mechanics* magazine has seven or more pages of classified advertisements. *Mother Earth News* magazine has a very healthy classified advertisement section and requires that all mail-order advertisers offer money-back guarantees to the buyers. In your own review of magazines, put the magazines that impress you in a folder, and you can include them in your media plan to be discussed later in the chapter.

Nothing replaces your own review of the magazine. How does the magazine feel in your hands? How is the color? Who is advertising in the magazine at this time? Does the magazine offer important information for the reader? Would you keep the magazine on your coffee table to review again in the future? Finally, ask yourself if this is a good publication to help you match your product or service to your target market.

STANDARD RATE AND DATA SERVICES

The *Standard Rate and Data* book is indispensable when you are choosing a magazine. It not only lists all magazines by title, it also includes addresses, phone numbers, and fax numbers. In addition, the publication summarizes the editorial content of the magazine. It includes the names of the key personnel and the representatives who sell advertisements for the publication. The *Standard Rate and Data* book also includes the advertising rates and whether a cash discount is offered for early payment, the rates for advertisements, classified advertising rates, and circulation of the magazines.

The value of the *Standard Rate and Data* is the opportunity to consider all magazines in a particular field. For example if you wanted to reach private schools, the publication would give you valuable information about the magazines servicing this market. There are data directories for radio, television, and newspapers, as well as information to help you prepare your media plan. Your local library or regional library will have a copy of this publication for you to use. Read through the directory and pick out magazines of interest to your customers. Write to the magazines and ask for a media kit and a copy of the publication.

THE MEDIA KIT

The media kit will include more complete information about the publications, including detailed demographics of subscribers, an audit statement showing the audience receiving the magazine, a rate card, editorial calendar, and other information.

The Editorial Calendar Can Help You Plan

In the media kit you will find an editorial calendar which is used to list the various subjects the magazine plans to cover in the following year. For example, *Writer's Digest* magazine offers a list of book publishers in July, August is devoted to articles and analysis of writing articles for women's magazines, and September is devoted to an analysis of writing novels and short stories. Choose a magazine that plans their campaigns to reach your target market.

The Magazine Rate Card

Each magazine offers a rate card that includes the title of the magazine, how many times a year issued, summary of the editorial content, circulation figures, advertising rates, classified rates, and closing time. The rate card is the summary of the publication. Review the rate card in Fig. 8-1.

Closing Dates

Magazines require that the advertisement is sent and paid for two or three months before the advertisement will run. For example, *Popular Science* magazine advertising closes on December 29 for the March issue the next year. When you plan to advertise in their magazine, consider the two-month wait.

1 PERSONNEL

Publisher and Advertising Manager—
  Harvey R. Kipen
Editor—Stan Holden
Production Manager—Betty C. Hinz

2 REPRESENTATIVES and/or BRANCH OFFICES

Chicago, Illinois 60611
Harvey R. Kipen
919 N. Michigan Avenue
Telephone (312) 787-4545

3 COMMISSION AND CASH DISCOUNT

a. 15% to recognized agencies.
b. 2% cash discount 10 days from date of invoice, net 30 days. No commission or discount on bills covering creative and mechanical services.
c. Bills rendered date mailing of an issue begins.

4 GENERAL

a. Rates subject to change without notice except on contracts which have been accepted and acknowledged by the publisher.
b. Advertising which is objectionable or misleading in the opinion of the publisher is not accepted.
c. Orders with special conditions such as positioning or editorial are not accepted.
d. No frequency discount.

5 DISPLAY ADVERTISING RATES

1 page (429 lines)	$2,450.00
2/3 page (286 lines)	1,845.00
1/2 page (214 lines)	1,590.00
1/3 page (143 lines)	1,150.00
1/6 page (70 lines)	595.00
1 inch (14 lines)	126.00
2 pages facing	4,765.00
2 pages facing, black and standard red	5,075.00

Advertisements other than standard units charged for on the following basis:

7- 69 lines	$9.00
71-142 lines	8.50
144-213 lines	8.00
215-285 lines	7.40
287-428 lines	6.45
Over 429 lines	5.70

6 COLOR

Red, per page, extra	$185.00
Red, smaller units, extra	155.00
Special color, per page, extra	250.00
Special color, smaller units, extra	225.00
Four colors, per page, extra	600.00

7 INSERTS

Post card	$3,950.00
First post card and ad page facing	6,550.00
Other post card positions with ad page facing	6,200.00
Add $155.00 for second color, standard red, page facing.

Post card inserts are 5" deep x 6" wide, printed in two colors, both sides.

8 BLEED

Bleed requirements: 8¾" wide x 11¼" deep. Type matter must be at least ¾" away from edge. No extra charge.

9 COVERS AND SPECIAL POSITIONS

Bigger space users get special positions on a rotating basis. No extra charge.

Split runs available. Information on request.

10 CLASSIFIED

$2.50 per word. Minimum 15 words—$37.50. First line set in Caps. All copy set solid without display, leaded or blank spaces. Name, address and numbers must be included in word count. Zip code does not count as word. Cash with order unless placed by recognized advertising agency.

11 CONTRACT AND COPY REGULATIONS

a. Advertisers and advertising agencies assume liability for all content of advertisements including text, representation and illustrations and also assume full liability for any claims against the publisher arising therefrom.
b. Cannot guarantee proofs for correction if copy is not received by closing date.
c. Publisher does not assume responsibility for errors in key number and no allowances or deductions are given should such errors occur.
d. Cash with order unless credit has been established.

12 MINIMUM DEPTH—ROP

1 column, 7 lines; double column, 14 lines.

Fig. 8-1. The magazine you choose is your personal vehicle to reach your chosen market. The rate card includes rates, closing times, and circulation information. Match the magazine with your product or service.

Newspapers require a much shorter waiting period; you can submit your advertisement on Monday and it's possible the newspaper can run it by Wednesday or Thursday. Some mail-order owners run advertisements in the newspaper first for a test, and then run them in magazines later.

SHOPPING OR MAIL-ORDER SECTIONS

Some magazines offer special rates to advertisers who will run advertisements in their special mail-order section. The mail-order sections offer products and services sold by mail. This section will give you an opportunity to place your product in a quality magazine with a quality readership in the millions.

ASK QUESTIONS

Write your advertising questions down as you review each magazine. In the media kit you will find the name and telephone number of the publisher's representative. Call or write the representative. Most earn their money on the commissions of advertisements they sell, so they will answer your questions.

PARTIAL CIRCULATION RATES

Special rates are offered to advertisers who want their product or service to reach only a specific group of people. For example, some medical journals sell advertisements by specialty. When you want to reach dentists, you would place your advertisement in a segment going to a dentist advertisement grouping. This partial group can offer you both good rates and a specialized audience.

REGIONAL RATES MAGAZINES

Some magazines can give you regional placement of your advertisement to help you focus on one part of the country. If your product is a warm-weather-related product, you would not want to try to sell it to colder climate sections of the country. This regional feature helps you to focus. Some mail-order owners advertise only to Florida and California. Now you are ready to prepare your media plan.

ASK OTHER ADVERTISERS

You can get valuable information about a magazine by asking other mail-order advertisers. Some mail-order people write to others in the field and simply ask them about a magazine. I had the experience of a mail-order owner writing to me to ask about a particular magazine. I gave him the answer, but each mail-order offer is unique—one offer might work in Publication A and fail miserably in Publication B. You must be willing to research a magazine, then try the magazine with your offer. The decision is up to you, but, remember, in mail order you must advertise on a continual basis or your customers or potential customers will forget about you. Keep your name and product in front of them at all times. You can achieve this by advertising continually, or you can take advantage of free advertising by giving out your own news release.

GET FREE ADVERTISING WITH YOUR OWN NEWS RELEASE

A news release is a carefully written message of usually one or two pages about your product or service. The news release offers information to the readers of magazines and newspapers, and the radio and television audience. All publications and broadcast outlets need information for their audiences. You can give them information in the form of a news release. A news release, also called a *publicity release*, must offer important information to the reader. It can tell why the product is worthwhile, how it works, how the product is made; it can even include the price, and the name and address of the mail-order company. (See Fig. 8-2.)

Most importantly, a news release must be factual and straightforward. It cannot be in the form of an advertisement telling the reader why your product is better than the competition. Save that for your brochure or your sales letter. If your news release is too much like an advertisement, the editor of the publication will throw it right in the wastepaper basket. After all, they *sell* information and advertisements. Why should they give you a free advertisement? They must set a precedent for all the other people who send news releases. Stick to the facts, and offer news.

Send off 50 to 100 news releases to get as much exposure as possible. Some mail-order people send 10 news releases out to various newspapers and magazines, and find they get only a small response. Once you send out the news release, continue to check future issues of the newspaper or magazine to see if they ran your release. Never call the newspaper or magazine to see if they ran the release, they are much too busy—they might remember your name and company and throw out all your future news releases. The secret in this business is to gain a reputation as a professional, build contacts, learn what works, and keep promoting yourself and your product or service.

You can get the names of the publications from the *Standard Rate and Data* book mentioned earlier in this chapter. Direct your letter to the editor of new products or services. Also, send a news release to your local newspaper and the other newspapers in your area. Don't hide your product or service away so no one knows about it. Send a release to your local radio or television station.

Include a photograph with your news release; this will give the editor of the magazine the opportunity to use it in news articles. A photograph can help you get your point across. Many mail-order owners find that they get more orders when they include a photo in their news releases. Glossy black and white photographs work very well. Using a combination of classified advertisements and news releases, their business increases at a steady pace.

NEWS RELEASE
for immediate use

----From NEW CAREER WAYS, William J. Bond, editor, 2 Margin Street, P.O.
Box 822, Salem MA   01970

A new exciting monthly newsletter, NEW CAREER WAYS, has just been released.
It is an unusually perceptive and down-to-earth letter, specially designed
to help the junior executive or executive operate and manage his or her
career successfully. To reach the top in your career, you must know the
relevant facts, figures, and new and practical ideas to help you in your
job. NEW CAREER WAYS offers you the information you require to stay ahead
in today's business world. Here are 11 new topics from NEW CAREER WAYS to
aid you in building tremendous success and wealth in your career:

    *How to get the raise you deserve.
    *How you can do your own career planning.
    *How you can receive constant respect from your employees.
    *How you can do more in less time.
    *How to deal with your key employee and secretary.
    *How you can adjust to the rapid technological and social changes.
    *How you can utilize your full potential and reach the top.
    *How to prepare your company for OSHA.
    *How you can put all your skills, talents, and abilities together.
    *How to use new ideas to become successful.
    *What special skills are required to succeed.

That's just a handful of the important subjects covered in NEW CAREER
WAYS Newsletter. It will also keep you up-to-date on new books, new
ways to deal with people, new methods of communication, how to get the
proper exposure on your job, and effective decision-making techniques.

A SPECIAL GIFT--FREE

You will receive a FREE copy of the recent report, "Minding Your Own
Time," which gives you 19 specific techniques to help you make better
use of your time. The ability to use your time correctly may spell the
difference between success and failure on the job. Yet this report is
yours FREE when you subscribe to NEW CAREER WAYS. A free sample copy
of NEW CAREER WAYS is enclosed. One year's subscription is $24.00.

Fig. 8-2. The news release is one of your most important methods to tell potential customers about your business and products or services. Many businesses receive orders from sending out news releases. Many newspapers and magazines depend on news releases for new ideas for their readers.

SEND YOUR NEWS RELEASE TO
NEWSLETTERS AND ASSOCIATIONS

Newsletter publishers succeed by delivering the latest information on a narrow specialty to their subscribers. For example, if you want to sell art supplies, send a news release to the newsletters aimed at artists. You can find this information in the *Directory of Associations* or the *Directory of Newsletters*—both are available at your library.

Sell your product or service at the association level as well. Send news releases and photographs to the associations devoted to artists. Keep trying to put your product under the sun to get the proper exposure for it. Remember the important statement my advertising director for a large Boston advertising agency said: "Every product has a place in the sun." Your main objective is to find it.

THE ADVERTISING AGENCY

Advertising agencies produce advertisements, develop advertising campaigns, and place your advertisements for you. Advertising agencies also perform research and do media plans. They can perform a single function for you or a full line of advertising functions. The advertising agency charges a fee, which includes the 15 percent commission on the cost of the advertisement. For example, if your advertisement is $100 the advertising agency will receive $15 for their commission.

The advertising agency is selling their expertise and their creative skills in writing the advertisement to sell their clients' products or services. The agency offers you specialized services to get your product to your target market. It will assign a writer to write your classified advertisement, display advertisement, or your sales letter and brochure.

I suggest you handle the preparation and placement of your advertisements yourself in the beginning. As you develop your business, you can consider using an advertising agency. Your advertising agency should have experience in mail order. Ask to see some of their mail-order advertisements, their sales letters, reply cards, and brochures. Spend some time in the agency to see if you feel comfortable with them. Mail order is a specialized business, and a knowledgeable advertising agency of mail order is essential to help you succeed.

REVIEW THE EDITORIAL FOCUS OF THE MAGAZINE

Magazines with strong readership have a specific editorial focus that appeals to a large amount of readers. Some magazines start with a strong focus and gain some success, but then change their editorial focus and fall behind in the circulation. A strong focus will deliver you the reader you are trying to sell in your mail-order business. For example, *Changing Times* magazine has a very strong editorial focus: it strives to give important information to help their readers purchase cars, phones, appliances, and even investments. A recent issue dealt with a full examination of colleges, and they carefully graded each one for their readers. Placing your ad in this type of magazine can be very effective and profitable for you.

TEST AND RETEST MAGAZINES

The best way to see whether or not your product or service will sell in a certain magazine is to run a test in that magazine. Never run one single advertisement and then quit if the advertisement fails to pull enough orders. Give the magazine a chance. Let the advertisement run two or three times to give the readers a chance to think over your offer. Some readers will read an advertisement two or three times before they buy or respond for more information.

BUY YOUR ADVERTISEMENTS IN A GROUP BUY

There are many ways to purchase advertisements for your business. One way is to buy a single classified advertisement from a single magazine. Another is to purchase an advertisement from a publisher who owns various publications and can include your advertisement in three or four magazines for a special rate. Check with the publisher to see whether or not they offer group buys. Group buys can be an excellent way to get additional advertising exposure for your product or service.

MAGAZINE ADVERTISING INCREASES INQUIRIES

The most important contribution magazine advertising, especially classified or small space advertising, offers is the opportunity to build your inquiry and customer list base. By developing a good list base you can send them other offers on a regular basis. Your list will be very important when you put a small catalog together. Your list, also called a *house list*, will be a very valuable part of your mail-order business.

TURN INQUIRIES INTO CUSTOMERS

Mail-order owners who succeed have the ability to turn inquiries from the people who are unsure whether they will buy into genuine sales of your product or service. You turn inquiries into customers by responding quickly with professional material, written in a motivating and persuasive manner. Too often mail-order people respond to customer inquiries too late, and their sales material is not convincing enough to sell properly. The next chapter will discuss this in greater detail.

MAGAZINE ADVERTISING IS COMPETITIVE

Try to make your classified advertisement or small-space advertisement stand out from the rest of the advertisements. Why run an advertisement that is similar to other advertisements in the magazine? Offer something in your advertisement to appeal to the reader of your advertisement. Are you offering free information? Tell them in your advertisement. Are you offering a free trial offer? Tell them about it.

DON'T COPY OTHERS

Just because a mail-order company uses the same advertisement over and over does not mean it will work for you. When you copy the advertisement, you may share the small response resulting from the sameness of the advertisements. Make a list of advertisements that attract your eye and your attention. Cut them out of the magazine, paste them on a plain sheet of paper, and place them in a folder for your own use as good advertisement ideas.

WHO IS READING THE MAGAZINE?

Check the media kit to fully analyze the people buying and reading the magazine. You can find where they live, where they work, and their income as well.

The publisher of one magazine offers the following analysis of its reading audience:

- 63.8% are college educated
- 60.3% earn more than $35,000.00 per year
- 53% are professional, technical, service or managerial
- 89% own their own homes
- 72% own two or more cars
- 51% have children in a private school or college

MAGAZINE ADVERTISEMENTS OFFER SELECTIVITY

Your magazine advertisement can be placed into the hands of specific places and people. When it reaches your best prospects, people who want to buy from you, orders are the result. For example, many mail-order companies advertise their goods and services in farm magazines. The strong buying power of the rural population is important to you. This rural market enjoys ordering products unavailable in their area. There are hundreds of farm publications that are read loyally from cover to cover, week after week, month after month.

MAGAZINE ADVERTISEMENTS START YOUR SELLING PROCESS

The key to successful magazine advertising is to advertise continually to keep selling the product. The sales start with the first advertisement and end with a carefully directed follow-up program with your sales literature. In the mail-order business you must continue to remind the reader or prospect of who you are, the name of your company, what your company stands for, your company's record and reputation (see Fig. 8-3). Keep selling your product or service from the advertisement to the sales literature. Your magazine is a salesperson for you; it opens the selling door to new customers.

Fig. 8-3. Magazine advertising opens the door for you to sell your mail-order product or service. The advertisements introduce your company, services, and products to potential customers so they can purchase quickly and easily. Steady advertising can build your reputation so you can start selling right away and build your house list.

GET THE FIGURES ON MAIL-ORDER PURCHASES

In your media kit you might also find information on the amount of mail-order purchases by the readers of the magazine. *Writer's Digest* magazine offers advertisers a reader-profile study of the products or services purchased by their readers. To purchase the best possible mail-order advertising requires asking many questions. When the publication shows readers with strong buying by mail, it warrants at least a test of a few advertisements. A breakdown of mail-order purchases by subscribers of *Writer's Digest* magazine is provided below.

Mail-Order Purchases

93% of *Writer's Digest* subscribers purchase both household and professional items through the mail.

*In the past 12 months, they ordered:

Books	64%
Adult clothing	39%
Records/tapes	35%
Gardening tools/seeds	20%
Writing supplies/equipment	18%
Investment/financial information or services	18%
Literary/publishing services	16%
Specialty food items	14%

*ADI Research—1986 Reader Profile Study

WHAT IS THE BEST MONTH TO ADVERTISE?

One of the best months to advertise is in February. Many mail-order people contend that this is because, in many areas, the weather is cold and snowy; readers are spending more time at home, and this increases their reading of magazines, newspapers, and catalogs. Other mail-order companies find that January, September, and October are their best months. Still others contend that November and March are their best months and business slows down in the summer. There are no absolutes. Much depends upon the product, service, and the publication.

People are buying all-year-round. People read magazines during the summer, and even take the magazines along with them on vacation. People buy gifts all-year-round. Some mail-order owners vary their advertisements in the interest of the buyer. For example, during the late fall, they may show how the product could be used as a Christmas gift. Gift products would do well before Christmas and drop off after the first of the year.

Advertise all-year-round. You need inquiries and orders to keep your business profitable. You cannot get the orders unless you advertise each month for the complete year. There are people who want to buy your product or service, so tell them about it.

DETERMINE THE COST PER INQUIRY

You can compare one magazine to another by determining the cost per inquiry. For example, let's say you ran a classified ad in *Popular Mechanics* and you paid $120. You received 200 inquiries for your advertisement during the next month. To determine your cost per inquiry, divide 200 into $120, and your answer is 60 cents. This is a very low-cost way to send your sales material to an interested mail-order buyer. Keep your inquiry cost down to increase your profits.

HOW FAST WILL THE INQUIRIES ARRIVE?

The inquiries will start a few days after the monthly publication is received in the mail by the subscribers. When your advertisement is new and appeals to the reader, expect 20 percent of your total inquiries the first week, 30 percent the next week, 30 percent the following week, and 10 percent during the next two weeks. The inquiries drop off when the next monthly magazine is delivered to subscribers. Your advertisement should be in the current issue as well. The subscribers will put aside the old issue and focus on the new one. Send information immediately to your inquiries. When you wait too long, the buyer turns to the next issue and responds to other attractive offers.

FOLLOW UP ON INQUIRIES

Send your best package once you receive an inquiry. The package may include a letter, brochure, order card, and reply envelope. The potential buyer is interested enough to respond to you for more information; pay special attention to get the sale. What if the inquirer fails to order your product or service? He just never responded to you. Since the potential customer invested some of his or her time and money to respond initially, you should send another package with a small change to get the order. Some mail-order people will give a lower price and stress the benefits of the product again. You may also try a third time to turn the inquiry into an order.

HAVE YOUR GOODS AVAILABLE

Only the foolhardy try to run a mail-order business without access to their products or services. If you get orders and inquiries, you must be able to service them. If you run out of products and expect to receive another shipment soon, write to your customer and inform him of the delay. Give the customer an opportunity to get his or her money back. Avoid real problems by informing your customers about the time of the shipment. Deliver on your promises and your services.

Here is an interesting poem on the business of mail order and the moral for advertisers.

Moral for Advertisers

A lion met a tiger
    As they drank beside a pool.
Said the tiger, ''Tell me why
    You're roaring like a fool.''
''That's not foolish,'' said the lion
    With a twinkle in his eyes.
''They call me king of all the beasts
    Because I advertise.''

A rabbit heard them talking,
    And ran home like a streak
He thought he'd try the lion's plan,
    But his roar was just a squeak.
A fox came to investigate—
    Had luncheon in the woods.
Moral: When you advertise, my friends,
    Be sure you've got the goods.
            —ANONYMOUS

USE DISPLAY ADVERTISING

Display advertising, an advertisement of one inch or more, can show more about your product than a classified advertisement. The real advantage of the display advertisement is the opportunity to test the reaction to your offer. By using a display advertisement you don't need the sales literature, such as a brochure, letter, and reply card. Tell your complete story in the display advertisement. Some mail-order people use a headline, photograph, and appealing copy to sell the products or services. Gear your advertisement based on the interest of the reader. Tell a complete story to get the order.

Some mail-order people try a display advertisement once their classified advertisement shows a profit. The display advertisement can give you more presence in the publication and help you get more orders and inquiries (see Fig. 8-4). One publisher from New York runs display advertisements in numerous business publications. The display advertisements include a strong headline, a photo of the book they are selling, and descriptive copy. The publishing company was willing to send a book to the customers on their approval, and then bill them for the book and the handling costs.

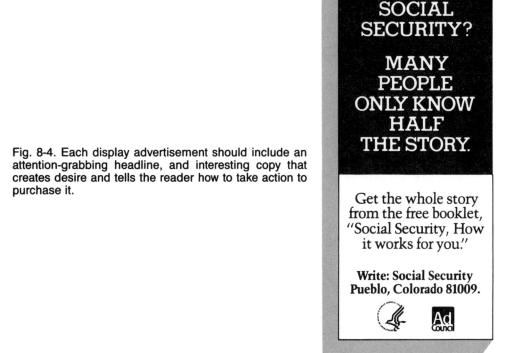

Fig. 8-4. Each display advertisement should include an attention-grabbing headline, and interesting copy that creates desire and tells the reader how to take action to purchase it.

HOW DO YOU KNOW WHICH INQUIRIES TURN INTO SALES?

The best method to determine where your inquiries are coming from is to key your advertisements. For example, at the end of your display or classified ad, where you list your company's name and address, you can include a department number next to the street, such as Dept. CL-A1, to show you advertised in January for the first month, and the magazine was *Popular Mechanics*. Keep a count of your inquiries. Once you send out your sales literature, write CL-A1 on the top right-hand corner of the reply card to show that this is the magazine that originated the inquiry.

Some magazines will deliver many inquiries, but result in few orders; others will offer fewer inquiries, but give you more orders. For example, say that during the month of January, you ran three classified advertisements in three different mail-order publications, and you used the two-step marketing method, whereby you followed up the inquiry with your sales literature to sell the inquiree. The results of your advertising program for January are on the following page.

Publication	Month	Key	No. of Inquiries	No. of Orders	% Orders versus Inq.
Popular Mechanics	Jan.	CL-A1	75	7	09.3%
Mother Earth News	Jan.	CL-B1	42	5	11.9%
Writer's Digest	Jan.	CL-C1	55	6	10.9%

The following is an example of an advertising profit projection.

Magazine Advertising Profit Projection

Mail Order Company	Jan.	Feb.	Mar.	Apr.	May	June	July	Aug.	Sep.	Oct.	Nov.	Dec.	Total Cost
A	$60	$60	$60	$60	$60	$60	$60	$60	$60	$60	$60	$60	$720
B			$75			$75			$75			$75	$300

	Company A	Company B
Sales	$1300	$430
Adv. & Product Costs	1050	366
Profit	$ 250	$ 64

Notice Company A received larger sales and profits because their advertisements appeared month after month. Company B also earned a profit by running four advertisements during the year. Notice the charge for Company A is $60, compared to $75 for Company B. The reason for the favorable advertising rate is the publisher offers a better rate when you advertise for a longer period of time. By advertising on a regular basis, you keep involved with handling inquiries, and this permits you to build your mailing list. Regular advertising keeps you in the mail-order game.

THE MEDIA PLAN IS YOUR ROADMAP

A media plan is a listing of the magazines you plan to use during the next year. The media plan will list the title of the magazine, the date of the issue, and the cost. Think a year, or even six months, ahead to help you complete the media plan. Visualize the cold December day while completing your media plan in the summer. A good media plan includes advertising on a steady basis during the whole year. Below you will find a media plan.

Publication Name	Date Scheduled	Closing Date	Type of Ad	Circulation	Ad Key	Cost
Popular Mechanics	January		Classified		CL-A1	$100
Mother Earth News	February		Classified		CL-B2	85
Writer's Digest	February		Classified		CL-C2	75

Publication Name	Date Scheduled	Closing Date	Type of Ad	Circulation	Ad Key	Cost
Popular Mechanics	March		Classified		CL-A3	100
Mother Earth News	April		Classified		CL-B4	85
Writer's Digest	May		Classified		CL-C5	75
Popular Mechanics	June		Classified		CL-C6	100
					TOTALS	$620

Keep a list of your inquiries and orders from each publication (see Fig. 8-5). Determine which publication or publications are earning money for you. During the next six months you can advertise more often in that publication. Give the readers a chance to consider your advertisements, then run your winners regularly.

In the following space I have included a blank media plan for your use. Fill your media plan out for a six-month period based on the publications you feel will best represent your product or service.

Your Media Plan

Publication Name	Date Scheduled	Closing Date	Type of Ad	Circulation	Ad Key	Cost

Media:	Per Wd. Minimum	KEY:
	Discount	CLASSIFICATION:
	Cost M	misc, personal
	Per Inch	ITEM:
D W BIM M SeM Q SA A	Minimum Discount	Sale Price:
	Cost M	Costs /1/adv.:
Circ:		App, gross :
	TF Class:yes no	
D/L _____ for _____	TF Disp: yes no	
Mail by :	Date Issued :	

date	no. wds.	Ad	no. iss.	totl pd.	cost iss.	iss. run	pt. rec.	renw by	c ✓	no. sales	gr. totl	P (L)		remarks

214 **** Have Printer enlarge this page 160% for 500 copies

Fig. 8-5. The media plan is important to help you develop a strategy for advertising for the full twelve months of the year. Too often mail-order owners advertise one month, and then wait to advertise again. With a two-month closing date, a media plan will help you develop a year-long program for success.

USING AN IN-HOUSE ADVERTISING AGENCY

Some mail-order people use an in-house advertising agency, which means they place their own advertisements using another name, for instance, the Smith Advertising Agency, and save the 15 percent commission. You might also get an extra 2 percent discount. The in-house advertising agency has a potential to save you 17 percent, but some magazines will not offer it to genuine advertising agencies. To use an in-house advertising agency you must use a name for the agency that is different from your mail-order business name.

HOW DO YOU SAVE MONEY?

You save on the agency commission offered to advertising agencies by the magazine publishers. For example, let's say you run an advertisement that costs $200. When you use an in-house advertising agency, your price would be only $170, the $200 less the advertising commission of 15 percent. Some magazine publishers also offer a 2 percent discount if the advertisement is paid within 10 days. Remember, not all magazine publishers accept the in-house advertisers, but some continue to accept them. Many magazine publishers do not give commissions on classified advertisements, they restrict their commission allowances to display advertisements. Now let's sum up magazine advertising.

SUMMARY OF KEY POINTS

- Select the magazines to reach the best-possible customers for your product or service.
- Get to know the circulation of the magazine.
- The Standard Rate and Data Service offers a listing of all publications, giving rates and other relevant information.
- The editorial calendar informs you of special editorial features during the coming year.
- The magazine rate card offers you the particulars of the magazine.
- The closing date is when the advertisement and payment is required for the advertisement.
- Some magazines offer a shipping or mail-order section, with special rates for you.
- Ask the right questions.
- There are partial circulation rates, and regional rates to reach a specific market.
- Use a news release and get *free* advertising. Send your news release to newsletters and associations to reach more of your market.

- The advertising agency performs a valuable service.
- Review the editorial tone of your magazine.
- Test your magazines.
- Buy your advertisements in a group buy.
- Magazine advertising often leads to inquiries—turn them into orders.
- Avoid copying others. Develop your own advertisements.
- Magazine advertising offers you selectivity. You can aim and hit your target market.
- Regular advertising means business for you.
- Determine the cost per inquiry. Your inquiries will follow a pattern. Give your inquiries fast, personable service. Make certain you have your goods or services available.
- Use display advertising.
- Keep a record of what inquiries turn into sales and what magazines are winners.
- Stay the course with a magazine.
- Project your profits.
- Your media plan is your plan for the future.
- You might save money with an in-house advertising agency.

9

Preparing Successful and Cost-Effective Sales Material

YOU ARE WHAT YOU CREATE IN YOUR POTENTIAL CUSTOMER'S MIND. YOU never get a second chance to create a good first impression. The potential customer will judge not only the words you use in your sales material, but also the look or image of your total selling package. Your mail-order business personality will leap off the page into the buyer's mind. When the buyer feels comfortable with your message, believes you, and reads enough of the material to make a decision, you will get the order.

The competition is tough. Many catalogs, offers, and sales letters are being sent to your potential customer, and only the most convincing offers will succeed. This chapter will give you ideas, strategies, and techniques to help you succeed.

ACHIEVE THE COMPETITIVE EDGE WITH PROFESSIONAL SALES MATERIAL

You must get the attention of your reader before you can make a sale. How often have you chosen one similar product over another based on the way the product was presented to you? In mail order you must beat your competition by presenting your product or service with attractive, professional sales material. The professional look includes an attractive logo, your full address, and phone number, in easy-to-read printing.

A logo is a way to identify your business; it helps the reader remember you and your business. A logo might be just the name of your company or a drawing of a lead product or a combination of both. Once you choose a logo, make certain it is on your sales letter, reply card, and your return envelope. Each element of your sales material should look like they belong to the same family. Your goal will be to prepare sales material that works so hard, each piece complements the other. Excellent sales material starts with excellent preparation and planning.

PREPARATION IS ESSENTIAL

Preparation is not only thinking about what things will be included in your material, but how it will look to the reader. For example, let's say you want to put some furniture into your living room to make it look better. Do you have the delivery person place the furniture in various parts of the room? Do you just hope and pray all pieces will fit into the room? What will you do if the sofa fails to fit in the left corner of the room? Why not make a layout or plan to put the various pieces into the right location? A lack of proper planning can spell disaster in almost every area of your life. Step back and spend the extra time to make certain your sales material will help you reach your goals and objectives.

PREPARE A LAYOUT

A layout is a plan for each piece of sales material so you can determine where the text and graphics are located. The text includes your words; the graphics includes any photographs, illustrations, charts, and diagrams. The layout is your attempt at a clear message to your reader. The layout starts with a clean sheet of paper and then moves in steps to the completed layout. Remember, there are several ways to organize your material on the page. Choose the best one. See Fig. 9-1 for an example of the different stages of a layout.

By doing a layout, you get a sense of the sales material—a feel for the message and whether or not your material will reach your target market. Your layout should highlight your product or service.

The reader has a specific eye flow. The reader will start reading at the upper left, move through the page, and end on the lower right corner. Research shows that readers like to look at photographs and illustrations first before they start to read the copy. A good combination of pictures in the form of photographs or drawings and copy can get your message across to your reader. An effective layout will make it easy for the reader to read the complete advertisement, and to take some action by ordering from you.

The layout must allow your product or service to look as good as possible. When your sales material looks professional, with excellent layout techniques, your material will have a positive visual effect on the reader. The different components of the advertisement or sales material, such as the headlines, photos, drawings, and copy, must work together and create an overall visual impact.

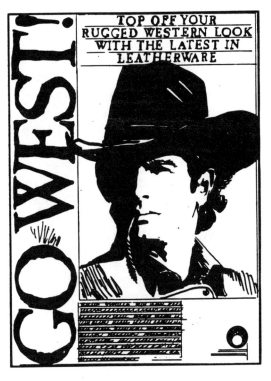

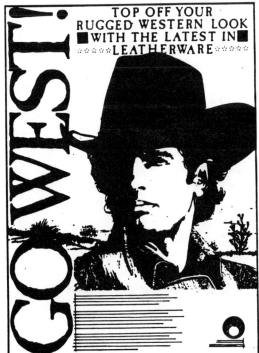

Fig. 9-1. This illustration shows you how a successful advertisement is developed, step by step from rough draft (upper left), to more complete layout (upper right), to the final stage (left), the comprehensive layout.

CHECK YOUR COPY

Did you describe the important benefits to your reader? Did you make your offer clear? Did you ask for the order? Too often sales are missed because the new mail-order entrepreneur did not ask for the order. Once your rough sales letter is completed, put it into an envelope and address it to yourself. If you want to save the cost of a postage stamp, drop it in your mailbox in the morning before the mailperson delivers your mail. When you check your mail, read your sales letter just like you are a potential customer. Did you enjoy reading it? Did it have an exciting message? Figure 9-2 gives you an idea what your sales letter will look like before you prepare it for printing. It is much easier to make copy corrections before the printing rather than after the printing. Proofread carefully.

TURNING YOUR WORDS INTO TYPE

The words you use on your sales material are very important; these words should be presented properly so the reader can understand your message. One way, and perhaps the easiest, is to type the words on your typewriter, or have a professional typing service do this for you. Make certain that the typewriter gives clear type; a printer cannot reproduce letters that are poorly formed because the ribbon on the typewriter is worn. Another option is to purchase *typography*, which is the process of setting and arranging typefaces, and printing from them. Typography is the design of the letter, produced by machine to be reproduced by printing. Some mail-order owners use a typewriter for most of their sales material and typographic design for their headlines. Your printer will show you various type styles, and you can choose the one you feel is easy to read, has a favorable appearance, and is appropriate for your sales material.

Obviously, a major difference between using a typewriter for your sales material and professional typography purchased from a printer is cost. You can have a page typed for $2 to $5 per page; if you purchased typography from the printer, it might cost $100 to $200 per page. However, when the printer sets type for you, you can get more words on one sheet than if you used a typewriter.

Laser type is developed by laser printers, charged by a pulsating light beam, which form letters with a powder into dots on paper. *Phototype* is produced by machines that employ laser beams that form characters on photosensitive paper. This system offers excellent quality and versatility.

Another important development in the typography field is the interfacing between computer and typography machines. For example, many phototype machines can read your copy from your computer disk, and set the type for your sales material. This is an important development, saving you a great deal of time and money.

Even if you use a typewriter, you can use a scanner that can read your type into a computer memory for your use. Some mail-order owners use their typewriter for their copy, but use specialized type for the headline. Use the typewriter and the phototype together to get a good result.

Choose the type that suits your sales material. When I started my mail-order business, I used my own typewriter to prepare the copy for all my sales material. I simply paid a professional typist to do the typing, and then I took the letter and material to the printer to print up the quantity needed.

CHOOSING A GOOD PRINTER

Your well-developed copy, your product idea, and your target market concept will die on the vine if you hire a printer who turns your sales material into an unprofessional and messy state of affairs. *You* make the decisions. You're in charge. Hire a printer who can deliver work that you will be proud to send to potential customers. Avoid the temptation of hiring the printer close to your home, or up the street from your place of employment merely because of convenience. Talk to other businesspeople who hire printers; ask them for a recommendation for a good printer. Look in your local telephone book for printers in your area. Find out what capacities are available in your local area. For example, I used one print shop for my sales letters, envelopes, reply cards, and reply envelopes. The price was good because I gave the printer the full job.

Printers vary in their capacities, quality, and price. Some printers have the capacity to do two-color printing, which means black and one other color, including blue, red, or green. Other printers specialize in business cards, stationery, brochures, advertising mailers, logos, typesetting, layout, and design. Visit print shops. Saturday morning is an ideal time. Be pleasant with your printer. In your own diplomatic fashion get across to your printer the product or service you want to sell in your mail-order business and the type of image you want to present. Printers need steady work to keep their business going, and many of them will be very helpful with ideas.

Look around the shop. Sample business cards, sales letters, and brochures are usually tacked up on the wall to give customers ideas and offer proof of their work. I make it a point to ask for samples of the work I plan to print. For example, I will ask for a recent sales letter, an envelope, and an order card. How does it look? Would you purchase a product or service from a company that sent out material similar to it? It will be up to you to set standards for your printing method. The potential customer in Minnesota reads your material and then makes a decision on your product or service. Give your potential customer confidence in you with quality printed material.

Can I share an exciting idea with you?

This idea is called "NEW CAREER WAYS," a unique newsletter, determined to offer you new ideas, methods, and strategies to assist you in your business and career. Every issue has your career success in mind. Every issue is concerned with increasing the profits of your business. Each issue is written in straight to-the-point language, giving you useful and practical advice to make you more successful in you career.

Whether you have just started your job or ~~whether you~~ have been working for three, four, ten, or more years, you can be more successful on your job. Almost everyone wants to succeed, but many people fail to achieve their goals for success. Some social scientists feel that the path towards success is a ~~par-ticular~~ process. It will be the primary function of NEW CAREER WAYS to describe this process so you can be more successful in your job. It involves: self-growth and development; establishing goals; knowledge of yourself, of your job, and of other people; leadership qualities; decision-making; use of time; executive success steps; and "Mr. Together," a description of an individual putting all the particular processes together.

A person's drive is essential to success on his job. Many social scientists contend that a person uses only a small fraction of his total abilities and talents. Personal drive is needed to get a better position, and to develop and grow. If you have personal drive, you will have the money you need to buy things for yourself and your family. A few people will be fortunate enough to win a substantial amount of money by simply buying a lottery ticket. Most people have to depend on their job as the only source of revenue to meet their financial obligations. When a person is armed with the knowledge of how to be successful on his job, and the personal drive to use that knowledge, he will be more successful. If you firmly believe you can be more effective and productive on your job--you will be. NEW CAREER WAYS can help you grow and develop. All successful people do!

Here, for example, is a rundown of the important subjects and questions that will be answered in NEW CAREER WAYS:

1. HOW TO DO MORE IN LESS TIME
2. HOW TO RECEIVE CONSTANT RESPECT FROM YOUR EMPLOYEES
3. HOW YOU CAN DO YOUR PERSONAL GROWTH PLAN-NING

Fig. 9-2. It will take time before your sales letter is written to your satisfaction. Write it, and then read it over again a day later. Read it as the potential customer. Make the necessary corrections until it is ready for typing or typesetting.

4. HOW TO DEAL WITH YOUR ~~RIGHT-HAND MAN~~ *KEY PERSON* AND
   YOUR SECRETARY

5. HOW TO PREPARE FOR OSHA

6. HOW TO USE YOUR FULL POTENTIAL

7. KNOWLEDGE CAN BE THE "SPECIAL KEY" TO MO-
   TIVATE YOURSELF AND OTHERS TO PRODUCE BETTER
   WORK

8. HOW ~~CAN I~~ *TO* ADJUST TO THE RAPID TECHNOLOGICAL
   AND SOCIAL CHANGES?

9. WHAT ARE THE SPECIAL SKILLS REQUIRED TO BE
   SUCCESSFUL ~~IN YOUR JOB~~?

10. HOW DO YOU PUT ALL YOUR SKILLS, TALENTS, AND
    ABILITIES TOGETHER AND BECOME "MR. TOGETHER?"

NEW CAREER WAYS will keep you up-to-date on new books, new ways
to handle people, and new methods of communication. Other areas of
concentration include: How to plan a personal health program,
how to get the proper exposure on your job, and how to make decisions.

This superlative newsletter is now being made available to you
at the special rate of just $2.00 a month, payable annually.

Simply fill out and mail the enclosed postpaid card, and I will
start your subscription to NEW CAREER WAYS at once.

                                        Cordially yours,

                                        William J. Bond

                                        William J. Bond
                                        Editor

WJB/cs

P.S. NEW CAREER WAYS will be an excellent investment in your
career or business. Don't delay -- fill out the attached
postcard today!

A SPECIAL GIFT -- All new subscribers will receive absolutely
free a copy of my booklet, "Minding Your Own Time."

Fig. 9-2. Continued.

DO ONE PRINTING JOB AT A TIME

Some mail-order owners cause their own printing nightmares because they try to print too many different jobs at the same time. Complete them one at a time. Complete your sales letter, first, then do your brochure or order card, and then you can finish up with your envelopes. By doing each project one at a time, you can handle the cost easier and you can concentrate fully to get the best results. Set up a time schedule, such as the one shown below. Make certain you have the material on-hand when your magazine or classified advertisement appears.

Time Schedule for Printing

Sales Material	Due Date
Sales letter	Jan. 10
Reply card	Jan. 17
Envelopes	Jan. 21

GET A QUOTATION FOR YOUR PRINTING

Try to get a written quotation from your printer for your printing. Verbal price quotes may work, but sometimes the printer forgets the quote, or he or she might give you different prices, and problems can result. Also, the printer may quote you on just the printing, and you might want some typography for your headlines. In this case, the final invoice will be higher than you expected. Doing a written quote forces you to think about exactly what you want printed. Figure 9-3 shows a quotation sheet for a two-page sales letter.

Once the printer receives your quote, he will fill out the bottom section to give you the amount for your records. Give the printer a self-addressed stamped envelope to speed up the delivery to you. Since you are just starting out with small quantities, your work will be faster by making it easier for your printer to respond to you. Before you send off your quotation request, remember to review it fully. Do you want your sales letter to be printed on both sides or on one side? Do you want white paper? Do you want it folded? Some mail-order people fold their own letters by hand just before they send out the material. What color ink do you want? What are you using for illustrations? Go over the quotation fully before you send it out. Make certain the quotation is the way you want it.

SET UP A BUDGET

By getting a written quotation from your printer, you can set up a budget for your printing work. Beginning mail-order owners make two basic mistakes when buying printing: they print too many copies, and they spend too much money for their printing. By using written quotations, you know what you will spend.

<u>Quotation For Printing</u>

Name __Cindy's Mail Order Co.____   Date ___Dec. 1, 1990___

Person to contact __Cindy McNeil_____   Phone _700-382-6119_

Address __67 Melrose Ave., New York, NY 10019_____

Job name ___Sales Letter_____

Number of pages ____2_____   Same side _____ yes __x__ no

Page size _81/2x11_ in. Folded size _31/3x81/2_ in. Quantity _1,000_

Date camera ready material to printer __Dec. 12_____

Date needed __Dec. 18_____

Paper weight _____ Color _____ Finish _____ Brand name _____

Ink colors _____ Front side _____ Other sides _____

Halftones _____ yes _____ no   Diagram _____

Illustration _____ yes _____ no   Drawing _____

Miscellaneous instructions _____

_____

** Quote for Printer

    My price for the above printing job, on date requested and
the quantity stated, including folding is $ _____ .

                          Signed _____

                          Date _____

                          Telephone _____

Fig. 9-3. A great deal of time is saved by mailing out your printing requirements for a quotation from various printers. You choose the printer based on the best quality for the best price.

One of the questions I am asked in my mail-order seminar is the cost to print up sales material. The cost will depend on a number of factors: the amount of copies printed, the color of the type, the amount of photographs, the amount of typography used, the grade of paper, and whether you print on one or two sides of the paper. My friend, Steve Maxam, recently printed up some sales material for his mail-order business. He printed a sales brochure with a photograph and two-color ink, a large 9 × 12 envelope, and a reply card including typography. For 1,000 copies he spent around $400. You may find that you can beat this price if your material is typed on your typewriter or computer, and you use one-color printing instead of the two colors. Purchase only the amount of printing you expect to use. You might want to make some changes in the next printing purchase, but when you purchase 5,000 or 10,000 copies, it will be very expensive to make the changes. Refer to the simple budget plan below for your printing job.

Budget for Printing Job

	Cost based on written quotations
1,000 Sales letters (2 pages)	_____
1,000 Brochures (1 side)	_____
1,000 Order cards	_____
1,000 Reply envelopes	_____
1,000 White envelopes	_____
TOTAL COST	_____

Some mail-order owners cut their printing costs on the reply envelopes by purchasing a rubber stamp with the company's name on it, and stamping the reply envelopes when they send them out. Some people put stamps on the reply envelopes to speed up the replies. Others ask the customer to use their own stamps.

MAKE USE OF YOUR PHOTOCOPY MACHINE

Sometimes the use of a photocopy machine can give you quick results when time is important. Let's say you receive some inquiries, and your printing job will not be completed for a week. The photocopy machine can give you quality reproductions quickly to get your material out to the inquiries. You must try to use clean originals, just like for printing, to get the best results. Some photocopy machines can reproduce almost as well as quick printing shops. Some photocopy machines do four-color copies.

TWO-COLOR AND FOUR-COLOR PRINTING

Two-color printing is attractive and can increase the professional look of your sales material. The fancy four-color material is very attractive, but costly. I suggest you use black ink on white or colored paper until your business grows to support the cost of four-color printing.

THE BASIC SALES MATERIAL FORMAT

I have found the best format to get orders in mail order is the sales letter, order card, reply envelope, and outside envelope. The sales letter is the salesperson in your sales package; it will stress the features of the product, and why the potential customer should buy it. It should be long enough to tell the full story to the reader. Some mail-order owners try to combine the sales letter and the reply card on the same sheet of paper. This might save some money, but it is much easier for the customer to write out the reply card when it is detached from the letter. Your job will be to make it as easy as possible for the reader of your sales material to order from you. In Fig. 9-4 you will find an example of a sales letter.

The reply or order card is designed to summarize the proposition you offer to the reader. It is very important because this is the first thing many people read when they open a sales package—they want to look at the price and get a quick summary of the offer, so they can make a quick decision. It must be attractive, easy to read, and stress the important selling points such as a money-back guarantee. A reply card is shown in Fig. 9-5.

The customer will use a reply envelope to send his or her order to you. When you request an order from your customer, the reply envelope is necessary so that he or she can enclose the check to pay for the order. The reply envelope will include the name and address of your company. In Fig. 9-6 you will find a sample of a reply envelope. Your reply envelope should be attractive but should look like other parts of the mailing.

The outside envelope that carries all the various pieces of your mailing package should look professional and attractive. It presents a good opportunity to start the selling process. One way to do this is to start the copy right on the envelope. Tell the customer the reasons why he or she should open the package and read it. Tell the customer how the product or service will save him time or earn him money. Tell the customer about the free offer inside.

A successful outside envelope includes your company's name and address on the left top corner of the envelope. The copy on the envelope should be a simple, but personal, message to the customer. The outside envelope should look similar to the rest of the package. An example of an outside envelope is shown in Fig. 9-7. Your outside envelope might be the most important part of your mailing package, since it is the first contact the customer will receive from you.

NEW CAREER WAYS
NEWSLETTER

NEW CAREER WAYS • 2 Margin St. • P.O. Box 822 • Salem, Mass. 01970

GREAT NEWS FOR TRAINING MANAGERS --

A TRAINING PROGRAM FOR 67¢ A MONTH

Dear Training Manager :

Success.

Isn't that what you're striving for?   Personal success. Success for your employees.

Obviously, you have the proper skills necessary, or else you wouldn't be where you are today.

But every single day -- new methods and techniques are being developed to help both you and your employees make better use of your skills, and thus be more successful.

And that's why I think you'd be interested in NEW CAREER WAYS NEWSLETTER, a new training approach for management. It's the inexpensive way to keep up with what's happening in today's business world.

NEW CAREER WAYS NEWSLETTER comes out each month with new articles, new ideas, and new business techniques to help you manage your time, your employees, your abilities -- so you can make as much money and be as successful as possible.

Not only will NEW CAREER WAYS NEWSLETTER be beneficial to you -- it will also be a great asset for your employees. It will train them to do their jobs more efficiently, so you'll obtain greater productivity from your organization.

NEW CAREER WAYS NEWSLETTER is one of the most successful training programs around for a number of reasons: (1) It's brief, so you learn a lot quickly (2) It's inexpensive, so you don't have to spend a great deal of money as with college courses (3) It's authoritative, so you'll know what's happening in business today and in the future (4) It's interesting, informative reading material that gives you information you can use directly on the job.

Fig. 9-4. Your sales letter is the salesperson in the buying process. Focus on the benefits of your product and why the buyer should purchase it. Use words to motivate your buyer to buy from you and take action right away.

All articles in NEW CAREER WAYS NEWSLETTER are well-researched and carefully planned. You'll receive information that's not available elsewhere. More facts, more figures, more successful techniques -- you'll get all this before your competitors.

ALREADY IN ITS THIRD YEAR

NEW CAREER WAYS NEWSLETTER has subscribers all over the country. Such companies as Dictaphone Corporation, First National Bank of Boston, Boston Mutual Insurance Co., Delco Electronics, Ryder Truck Rental, Intertel Communications Corp., Paul Revere Life Insurance Co., Naumkeag Trust Co., Travelers Insurance Co., Bay State National Bank, and many others use NEW CAREER WAYS NEWSLETTER as part of their management training program. And all of them are extremely pleased:

"Thank you for your recent issue, "How To Cut Your Workload and Accomplish More". I learned some vital techniques to get things done through other people. Your newsletter is informative and keeps me motivated."

R. Wilson, President
Pembrook Soda Co., Pembrook, Mass.

"I learned some valuable facts from your issue, "How To Prepare For OSHA". I will save hundreds of dollars and I now understand much more about this law."

P. Sine, Vice President
Sine Construction Co., Bradenton, Fla.

"Your newsletter appears to be extremely valuable. After 13 years of editing (Academic Business Journals), I have concluded that newsletters are the way to reach managers."

W. G. Ryan, Executive Editor
Business Horizons, Bloomington, Indiana

WHAT THE BUSINESS MAGAZINES ARE SAYING ABOUT NEW CAREER WAYS NEWSLETTER:

THE NATIONAL PUBLIC ACCOUNTANT even said it was "an unusually perceptive and down-to-earth newsletter especially designed to help the junior executive or executive operate and manage his or her career successfully."

THE FLORIDA BUSINESS DIGEST even said: "an excellent way to keep up to date on new business techniques -- and helping you to move ahead in your business career."

Fig. 9-4. Continued. Second page of New Career Ways newsletter.

ABOUT THE EDITOR

WILLIAM J. BOND, Editor of NEW CAREER WAYS NEWSLETTER is a Business Consultant. He holds a Master of Arts degree and Bachelor of Science degree from Salem State College. Mr. Bond has written widely in professional journals such as THE NATIONAL PUBLIC ACCOUNTANT, TEXAS CPA, THE AMERICAN CHAMBER OF COMMERCE and EXECUTIVE JOURNAL. He is also a columnist for FLORIDA BUSINESS JOURNAL and EXECUTIVE REVIEW MAGAZINE. He has written a book, and is presently working on a second book. Mr. Bond resides in Haverhill, Mass.

EACH ISSUE CONTAINS ON THE JOB MATERIAL

What makes NEW CAREER WAYS NEWSLETTER so unique is that each article is written in down-to-earth language, and gives important pointers on how to do a better job. Here are a few examples of some of the previous articles:

"... Be sure you take advantage of the credit for personal exemptions on your income tax. As part of the new tax package approved by Congress this year, you will receive $30 for each one of your personal exemptions. This credit will be deducted from the total tax owed on line 16b of your form 1040 ..." From the article, "Your 1976 Income Tax Report".

"... Paperwork can be a great time waster and it accounts for a large part of your workload. Try to handle each piece of paper once. If you cannot use it, try to put it in the waste basket. Update your files as often as necessary; clean out all unnecessary papers ..." From the article, "How to Cut Your Workload and Accomplish More".

"... Women play a very important role in any business or organization. It's up to both women and men to make certain that all employees get the proper opportunities to show their talents and abilities. When all employees are operating at top efficiency, it makes for a more productive and successful organization ..." From the article, "New Career Opportunities For Women".

Fig. 9-4. Continued. Third page of New Career Ways newsletter.

FUTURE ISSUES

Some of the articles to be covered in the next 12 issues are:

1. How to Cut Your Business Expenses

2. How You Can Do More In Less Time

3. How You Can Put All Your Skills, Talents, And Abilities Together

4. How You Can Successfully Handle People

5. How To Write Better Letters, Memos, Reports and Analyses

MONEY BACK GUARANTEE

If for any reason you are not satisfied with NEW CAREER WAYS NEWSLETTER, you can stop your subscription at any time, and the unused portion of your money will be completely refunded.

AT AN UNBELIEVABLE LOW PRICE

Your subscription to NEW CAREER·WAYS NEWSLETTER will cost you just $24. But, every subscription thereafter (for supervisory personnel) will cost only $8.

SPECIAL GIFT

If you subscribe within the next 10 days, we will send you the special report, "Minding Your Own Time". This valuable study contains 20 new techniques to help you save time in order to do your work more efficiently. It is read by businessmen all over the country.

SUBSCRIBE TODAY

NEW CAREER WAYS NEWSLETTER will help you immediately. So don't put it off ! Order today, and receive your first issue almost immediately.

Then you'll be a better career person tomorrow.

Sincerely,

William Bond

William Bond
Editor-in-Chief

WB/sdb

Fig. 9-4. Continued. Final page of New Career Ways newsletter.

Check and return this form promptly

NEW CAREER WAYS
P.O.Box 822 ● 2 Margin St. ● Salem, Mass. 01970

Circulated to business clients monthly...

YES, sign me up for **NEW CAREER WAYS** Newsletter at the special charter rate of $2.00 a month payable annually. (This special offer includes the exciting executive report "Minding Your Own Time" FREE)

Send us_____ additional copies at $8 per year each for distribution to our supervisory personnel (all to same location).

☐ Bill Company   ☐ Bill Me   ☐ Check enclosed

Company_____

Name_____Title_____

Address_____

City_____ State_____Zip_____

Make check payable to **NEW CAREER WAYS**

REFUND GUARANTEE: The unused portion of your payment will be returned to you on request at any time.

Fig. 9-5. The reply card is your salesperson summarizing your offer and making it easy for the buyer to act. Your potential customer will read your reply card often before ordering. Include important selling points such as price, guarantee, shipping and handling costs.

First Class
U.S. Postage
PAID
Permit No. 1037
Salem, MA 01970

BUSINESS REPLY MAIL
No postage stamp necessary if mailed in the United States

Postage will be paid by

NEW CAREER WAYS
NEWSLETTER

2 Margin Street
P.O. Box 822
Salem, Massachusetts 01970

Fig. 9-6. Match your reply envelope with your reply card. Tell the potential customer the reply envelope is enclosed to make it easy to send the order.

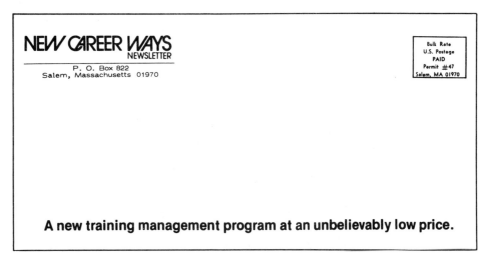

NEW CAREER WAYS
NEWSLETTER
P. O. Box 822
Salem, Massachusetts 01970

Bulk Rate
U.S. Postage
PAID
Permit #47
Salem, MA 01970

A new training management program at an unbelievably low price.

Fig. 9-7. The role of your outside envelope is to attract enough attention to open it. Nothing happens until your information is opened, fully read, and then the order is given to you.

CHECKLIST FOR ACCEPTANCE OF YOUR PRINTING

You called the printer and they told you to pick up the printing on Saturday morning. The mistake many mail-order owners make is picking up the printing work quickly without carefully reviewing the work. It doesn't matter whether you pay on delivery or the printer invoices you for the work, never pay for anything until it meets your approval. It is a good idea to bring the written quotation with you when you pick up the work to compare the price on the bill and your quote. When the invoice or bill is more than the quote, find out from the printer the reason for the difference. When you make changes after the original quote was given, such as extra typography or extra colors, the price will be higher. Also look carefully at all of the copies; sometimes a printer will put the best copies on the top of the pile, and halfway down the pile the quality goes down and the ink is smudged. When a bill is presented to you, read it over, check the arithmetic, and if there is a mistake, let the printer know about it so he can make the correction. Demand quality, but remember, the printer is in business to make money just like you. Be firm but be as diplomatic as possible. A good dependable printer is a very valuable part of your business. Refer to the list on p. 108 for items to review at the printer's before you accept your printing job.

When the printer finishes the job on time and presents you excellent work in line with the quotation, remember to thank him and try to use this printer in the future. Once you find a printer who understands you and your business, it wills save you time and money.

Checklist for the Delivered Job

Yes	No	
____	____	Does the printing quality meet your requirements?
____	____	Did they use the paper you selected?
____	____	Did they include the art work or photography?
____	____	Make certain the printer gives you the right quantity. Count them.
____	____	Check the bill for accuracy.
____	____	Ask the printer whether or not you can do something more in the preparation to make the job look even better.

SUMMARY OF KEY POINTS

- Mail your offer to your target market such as teachers, chain operators, doctors, VCR owners, or salespeople.
- With the sales material, you can now tell your story to others.
- Choose your potential customer with care, it is expensive to print up and mail your mailing package.
- The key to successful, attractive, and reasonably priced sales materials is knowing exactly what you want, and then working closely with the printer to get the best results.
- Start with a rough layout, review your copy carefully, keep your changes to a minimum, get the quotation signed by the printer, and examine the work before you pick it up.

10

Customer Service

DO YOU KNOW THE NUMBER ONE REASON WHY MAIL-ORDER COMPANIES ATTRACT new customers? By giving the best possible service. L.L. Bean, a leading mail-order company, gives individual attention to each customer.

You spent your hard-earned money to advertise your product or service and to purchase sales material. Now the potential buyer sends you a letter or post-card for more information. It is important to respond back to your potential buyer as soon as possible. Why? Your potential buyer was interested enough in your product or service to take the time to write to you for more information. Strike when the iron is hot. Send your sales material immediately to get the response you need.

ANALYZE THE INQUIRY

Your ability to handle inquiries well can make your business succeed. The inquiries are the lifeblood of your business. Each inquiry gives you information about the type of customer asking about your product. For example, what magazine advertisement brought in the inquiry? What classification did you use to classify the advertisement? Did you place the advertisement in "books and publications," "business opportunities," or "business services?" Did the inquiry result from a satisfied customer? Did the inquiry result from an article in a magazine or newspaper? All of this information is valuable for future advertising.

Set up an Area to Handle Inquiries

Inquiries are so important a separate desk or area should be developed in your office to handle them. For example, when you set up a separate desk, keep your sales materials in this desk as well. You want to locate the postage stamps and envelopes in the same desk so you can turn the inquiry into a mailing package to respond to the potential customer.

Determine What the Customer Needs

Read the inquiry and determine just what the potential customer needs. Does he want information on your new product? Does he need information on your prices? Does he need information on your guarantee? Will your complete selling package answer all the questions? Send the right information to your customer.

Treat All Inquiries with Care

Everyone has the potential to be a purchaser of your product or service. When he receives your sales material on a timely basis, and it answers all his questions, the chances of buying from you increases. This customer is a king, and the potential customer is potential royalty. Never forget it.

Time Is Important

The adage "Time Is Money" applies here: the faster you can get the information to the potential customer, the higher your response will be to your offer. When you keep the customer waiting, the competition sends him information and you may lose the sale. When you wait two or three weeks, the potential customer may forget about responding to you. Make it a rule in your business to respond within 24 hours—48 hours at the very latest.

Set an Inquiry Goal Daily

Mail your inquiries daily. Set a goal to send 50 inquiries out daily. If you only get 35 inquiries today, send out 15 offers to your customers who purchased from you last month. If Josephine Smith bought product A from you in December, send information on product B in January. The key to a successful business is converting inquiries into customers.

Make an Inquiry Record

The inquiry system is not only necessary to get your product or service sold, it also gives you an opportunity to determine who is buying, what they are buying, and what magazine is bringing in the sales. An inquiry record can help you do the follow-up sales as well. Let's say you received an inquiry for your manual on building a family room from Paula Smithurst of New York who responded to your classified ad in *Popular Mechanics*. Your plan is to send her a sales letter, brochure, order card, and reply envelope to make the sale. You will guarantee it fully. Now, how will you know that this inquiry from Paula Smithurst resulted from the advertisement in *Popular Mechanics*? Good question. Your advertisement included your address as: 39PM Millville Avenue, Stoneyville, Alabama. The PM after the 39 represents the key to identify the magazine. Many mail-order people understand the keying method but fail to use it fully. They begin to write notes on the envelope to identify the package sent, date, and follow-up. Once the initial package is sent, it is difficult to reconstruct the paper work again. A better way would be to use an inquiry record.

In Fig. 10-1 you will find an inquiry record for your mail-order business. It is very important in the beginning to use an inquiry record system for all inquiries

```
NAME_____

ADDRESS_____

CITY_____STATE_____ ZIP_____

                                                    DATE
DATE                                 MATERIAL     FOLLOW-UP
REC'D    MAGAZINE    ADVERTISEMENT     SHIPPED     MATERIAL
_____    _____    _____    _____     _____


         DATE
         ORDER
         RECEIVED        NO.           VALUE
         _____     _____      $_____
         _____     _____      $_____
         _____     _____      $_____

PRODUCTS OF INTEREST_____

DATE ENTERED ON MAILING LIST_____

REMARKS_____

WILL FOLLOW UP AGAIN_____
```

Fig. 10-1. Each sale represents a new inquiry record or an addition to the record. This gives you a full history of how the inquiry was made, the advertisement used, which magazine, amount of order, and follow-up. This record shows trends and changes in your business. Keep these records up-to-date.

because it will give you information on what magazines are giving you the inquiries and the orders. The inquiry record gives you the information necessary to start your own mailing list. The heart and soul of your mail-order business is your list of customers, and the best way you can develop it will be by a good, accurate inquiry system. We will discuss how to rent a mailing list in the next chapter, but your own list will be very valuable to you in the future.

You can keep these inquiry cards in a file cabinet or on computer disk in your office. Use them to determine what percentage of inquiries are converted into sales. For example, let's say you receive 200 inquiries and 20 are converted into sales, the percentage would be 10 percent. The inquiry cards can also give you information on the magazine that generated the sales for the period. An example is the analysis for the month of January.

Inquiries	Number Converted	Percentage	Magazines
200	20	10%	10 magazines A
			6 magazines B
			4 magazines C

Your inquiry card could also determine the amount of follow-up required to reach a sale. For example, some mail-order owners send out a package a month following the first mailing. Others send a total of three mailings spaced three weeks apart to try to persuade the potential buyer to purchase the product.

CODING ADVERTISEMENTS AND MAGAZINES

When you send your sales material to an inquirer, on the right-hand corner of the order card you can write PM-12 to signify that this inquiry was from your advertisement in *Popular Mechanics*, which ran in the December issue. Make sure that each order card is keyed accurately to give you the important information.

TELL YOUR EMPLOYEES ABOUT YOUR SYSTEM

You may set up the inquiry system yourself, and you know how to use it fully, but what happens when you come down with the flu or have to be out for a few days? Will you be forced to wait until you return? Give this information to other family members or employees to keep your business going. For example, include the following on a sheet of paper and tape it to the wall above the inquiry desk.

Inquiry System

Product—   Family Room Manual

Materials—   Sales letter, brochure, reply envelope, reply card, #10 envelope

Mailing—   First class; within 24 – 48 hours
Key—   Order card
Inquiry Card— Fill out completely

TOO MANY INQUIRIES

One mail-order owner in Maine was getting too many inquiries from his classified advertisements in mail-order magazines. When he examined his advertisements, he was not screening out his audience enough and was giving away free sample products. When you give away samples, expect to increase your inquiries, not necessarily the percentage converted to sales. Your goal is not casual inquirers, but qualified inquirers ready to buy from you. "Qualified inquirers" refers to people, including business organizations, with sufficient money and desire to buy your product or service. Too many inquiries are better than too few, but you must look carefully at the cost to fulfill the inquiries and the sales that result from them.

MULTIPLE INQUIRIES FROM THE SAME PERSON

During your first few months in the business, you will be looking carefully at all your inquiries from your advertisements. You might notice Mary Smith in Penola, Florida asking for information on your product two or three times. Some customers read your advertisement in two different magazines, or simply send you two letters by mistake. Your inquiry card can help you uncover this duplication. Some people, including businesses and organizations, enjoy sending for information in their field of interest. You must decide whether it is profitable to continue to send this information to the same people without a sale. I had one inquirer from New York who would respond three or four times to different advertisements—then I received three or four inquiries with the same name from Florida. I found out later that, each year, he spends three or four months in Florida and then moves back to New York.

TREAT YOUR INQUIRIES EQUALLY

Your inquiries will come to you in all forms: typewritten letters, hand written letters, postcards, and small and large envelopes. Send them all the same package unless there is a special request. The individual who sent the postcard might be one of your best customers, and the person who sent a well-written letter on fancy stationery might never respond to you again. Treat them all the same and watch for your results.

BE FRIENDLY AND POLITE

Your job will be to pull a nice red carpet down so you can deliver the best-looking sales package available to the potential customer. Give each customer special attention. Be friendly, all inquiries are special. Be polite, potential customers have a right to be fussy, and, after all, they are being courted by the competition as well.

FAST METHOD FOR HANDLING INQUIRIES

Some mail-order owners want to get their message out quickly, so they simply cut out the name and answer from the letter, tape it to the envelope they send out, include their sales material in the envelope, and send it to the inquirer. You can then use the name and address from the inquirer's envelope to add to your mailing list.

OTHER SOURCES OF INQUIRIES

Most of your inquiries will be a result of your advertising in magazines, but other sources are available as well. A well-planned news release to various publications, including newsletters, association publications, magazines, and newspapers can increase inquiries and sometimes direct sales. I had the happy experience of getting a newsletter to talk about a manual I was selling and I received a number of inquiries and sales.

There are other ways to get inquiries as well. One is to appear on a talk-radio program to talk about your business, your product, and yourself. People want to hear about a new product, and nothing is more exciting than to hear it from an owner of the business. For example, I appeared on a large talk-radio program based in Boston, but which reached 40 states and a large part of Canada, and talked about my business. There was interest in the show and the host asked me to take calls from the listeners from all over the country. One call was from Maine, another from Georgia, another from Michigan. It became a country-wide seminar on home-business ideas.

It was a night program and getting late. I visualized people falling asleep, or turning their radios off to prepare for bed. I asked the host if I could give my address to the listeners to give them some free information. The host was happy to let me do this for his listeners. So I said over the air, "I will be happy to send you a new report on home businesses if you send me a *large* self-addressed stamped envelope to Bill Bond, P.O. #1, Haverhill, Massachusetts 01830." I repeated the name and address to help the people trying to get a pen and paper to write it down. I went back to taking questions, and finished up the show at 2 o'clock in the morning.

A few days later I went to the post office and checked my mail. It was filled with stacks of mail from all over the country. The letters arrived from Maine to

California—almost everyone had a self-addressed stamped envelope, so I could save a great deal of time and money. I received a number of orders from these inquiries and added them to my mailing list. The phone also rang steadily for the next few days with people asking questions about the show.

I appeared on the radio before this huge success, but I never asked the listeners to respond for this free report offer. Use that sales material you prepared for your business. People will send you a self-addressed stamped envelope if you will send them something of value in return. I also asked for a *large* envelope, because if they sent small, 3- × -5 inch envelopes, it would be impossible to send the report and other offers to them. When you send back the report, include your sales material for your products so that you can add to your sales.

You may also try to appear on your local television shows for added exposure and inquiries. Your local cable station offers many opportunities to talk about your products, your services, and your business. You might even consider starting your own show if you have the desire and the time to do so. The more promotion you receive, especially free promotion and exposure, will give you and your business more inquiries, sales, and profits. I have appeared on many television shows and each show gave me a chance to reach people outside the normal mail-order circle of my business. Succeeding in mail-order requires a creative outlook on promotions for your business.

HOW DO YOU GET ON A RADIO AND TELEVISION SHOW?

Write a letter to the program director of the show. Tell the program director why you feel your idea will benefit their audience. In your letter, focus not on how *you* can benefit, but how the general public and their listeners or viewers will benefit. Will the public learn more about refinishing their family room? Will the public learn more about crafts? Will the public know more about how to purchase children's clothes? Show the program director you are knowledgeable about your subject and want to give information to the public. All television and radio stations are licensed to have shows and programs to help the public. Once you send the letter, wait a week or two for a reply. If you fail to get a response, call the station and talk with the program manager about your availability. Keep trying until you get booked for the show. Once you get on a few shows, you will feel more relaxed and then receive additional offers to do other shows.

SUCCESS BREEDS SUCCESS

When you handle your inquirers professionally and offer an attractive sales package with an exciting offer, you will reach success. Once you're successful in this two-step marketing program, you can now begin to plan your own direct-mailing program with our own mailing list and others. We will discuss these important subjects in the next chapter.

SUMMARY OF KEY POINTS

- Your inquiry system is just as important as the selection of your product, your advertising, your target market, or any other element in your business. If you neglect it, the potential customer will view you and your business as profit orientated and sadly lacking in service or concern about the customer.

- Your inquiry system must be done correctly, on time, and be well documented so you know what advertisements are working, what magazines are working, and what follow-up is required to turn an inquirer into a customer.

- Your success will depend upon your ability to turn an inquirer into a member of your mail-order family—a customer of your business. Once he or she buys a product from you, your job will be to keep that customer buying over and over again in the future.

11

Selecting Mailing Lists

I RECALL VIVIDLY A CONVERSATION WITH A FRIEND WHEN I FIRST STARTED MY mail-order business 15 years ago. I told my friend I rented a mailing list to reach some potential new customers to sell my publication. My friend replied quickly, "Why do you spend money like that? Just take the names out of your local telephone book." To make your mailing work will require the best names possible, not someone out of your local phone book who never heard of you, your product or service, or your company in the past. A mailing list is like a good salesperson; it is neat in appearance, well organized, and offers a great deal of valuable information about your potential customers.

WHAT IS THE BEST POSSIBLE LIST?

The best possible list is your own list (also called a *house list*) of the customers who not only inquired about your product, but purchased a product from you. These customers know you, your product, and your company. They are special because they purchased from you. Build your business by keeping your house list up-to-date and continue to use it by a regular mailing of offers to them. Some mail-order owners include their inquiries on their house list. It is better to keep the buying customers separate from your inquirers. The response will be stronger from your own house list, than from any other list you can use. You might also want to rent it out for additional profits in the future.

MAIL-RESPONSE LIST

A *mail-response list* is a list you rent, not buy, from another company, perhaps in the same field as yourself, for a set price of, say, $75 per thousand names. You rent their house list. Let's say you want to expand sales of your "Family Room" construction manual, and you have mailed to all your inquirers. Why rent names from a competitor? Because the people on their list represent people who purchased by mail a manual on constructing other buildings and rooms in the past. These people have qualified themselves by purchasing other construction publications for at least $19.95 during the past six months. The people on this list could be called "hot-line" buyers because they purchased a similar product to yours during the last six months. Some mail-response lists are better than others, but all give you an opportunity to expand your customer base and increase your sales.

COMPILED LIST

A *compiled list* is a list of names you gather by taking them out of newspaper clippings, sales records, a city directory, association trade show lists, a voters' list, a telephone book, and so on. Some mail-order owners use auto registration lists to sell their auto-related products, such as mirrors, floor mats, and tape decks, to newly registered car owners. Many mail-order people are creatively using the compiled lists and further classifying them by age, geographic location, and amount of purchase to design a list of very qualified and ready-to-purchase buyers. Be sure to test compiled lists before spending the time and money needed to compile it.

WHAT SHOULD A LIST DO FOR YOU?

A list should sell more products and services. Postage is very expensive today. Preparing and printing sales material is costly. You cannot afford to send your offers to people who lack the interest or purchasing power. A list should be accurate and should give you the correct name of the person, the correct address, and the right zip code. The names should be fresh. The older the names, the poorer the response. For example, if someone on your list purchased a product two years ago, it will not be as strong as a name who purchased a product three months ago. A good list gives you the ability to put your offer to a ready-and-willing buyer.

LIST RENTAL

You want to expand your sales, so you decide to buy a list to get additional names. Sorry, but very few mail-order companies will sell you their names. Instead, they will rent you their names for a one-time use only, which you cannot copy, for a set price per thousand names. For example, let's say you want to rent the subscribers to *Fortune* magazine to sell them your product or service. *Fortune* magazine will rent to you, for a one-time use only, a list of names for a price of $70 per thousand names. *Fortune* magazine can increase their business sales by renting out their list to other mailers. Once the customer buys from you or communicates to you by telephone or letter, then the customer's name is yours to use.

LIST BROKERS

A *list broker* is a list consultant who will offer suggestions for possible list rentals for your business. They get paid a commission from the list owner. List brokers will examine your customers and develop a profile of them, including their age, income, occupation, geographic location, lifestyle, and other important factors. Once the list broker develops this profile and analyzes your product or service, he or she will make list rental recommendations to you. You will make the final decision on what list you choose to rent. The list broker will coordinate the paperwork and the delivery of your rental list at the proper time and place for your mailing.

The mailing list broker should know the performance of the list he or she recommends to you. The broker should also know the new lists coming into the list rental market. He or she will tell you how often the list is cleaned. Your mailing-list broker is your consultant, use his or her knowledge to the maximum. You can find a list broker through a recommendation of a friend or from your phone book under mailing lists or direct mail.

LISTS AGE QUICKLY

A list is like a salesperson. If the salesperson does not take care of his or her health and works excessively hard, there will be some aging. Your list will act the same way if it is not cleaned regularly. It will not do the job automatically to earn profits for your business.

To keep your list healthy, or to rent a healthy list, requires the use of constant updating to keep the names and addresses accurate. One way is to ask the people on your list to check the name and address on the label to see if there are any changes. Any changes should be noted and corrected right away. For a fee, the postal service will also correct the old addresses for you. If you print "Address Correction Requested" on the upper-left-hand corner of your envelope under your name and address, the post office will give you the new address.

Another method to keep your names up-to-date and avoid duplication of names is the "merge-and-purge system." This system is best suited for mail-order businesses with their names on magnetic tapes or punch cards. It has the ability to compare the names on your own list with the names on the rented list, with all the other lists in the mailing-list service organization. This system tries to cut out the names which get on many lists. No matter how many names are required, you will receive one set of labels without duplication between your rented list and your own house list. This merge-and-purge system can save you many thousands of dollars when you rent lists on a regular basis. Prior to renting a list, ask your list broker whether or not the merge-and-purge system is used.

When your mailing-list company uses the merge-and-purge system, ask about a list of the names that appear on two or more lists. You might find these names to be profitable because they are known mail-order buyers. They enjoy receiving mail and reading new offers. In marketing terms, these names are called "heavy users," and purchase a large percentage of the mail-order products and services offered each year. Some mail-order owners mail out to these heavy users two or three times.

Should you rent your list or not? I do not recommend renting your list in the first or second year of your business. You need these names to sell your own products or services. Once you build your list to a substantial number, such as 25,000 to 35,000 names, it will be a very valuable profit center for you. Many mail-order owners find extra profits in their list rentals. You might consider doing the same at the proper time.

KEEP YOUR LIST SECURE

Just as you do not permit anyone to take the keys for your home or your apartment, the same applies to your list of customers or inquiries. Too much money and effort has been spent on these names; do not let others use them without your permission. Some mail-order owners lock their mailing list in a safe, others will use a file with only one key solely for the owner of the business. Other mail-order people will not permit mailing-list cards, disks, or tapes to leave the company without approved shipping receipts. You must show a genuine interest in the security of your list to show others within your home or organization the value of your list.

WHAT LISTS ARE AVAILABLE TO RENT?

Thousands of lists are available. With the computer and creative programming you can select a list of very high quality to sell your product or service. For example, let's say you want to sell your product or service to a food manufacturer. Since there are over 23,000 food manufacturers, you can narrow it down to one type of food manufacturer, such as meat-packing, coffee, or macaroni manufacturers. In Fig. 11-1 you will find a list of food manufacturers in the United States.

S.I.C.	Description	Count for U.S.
2000	Food & Kindred products mfrs.	23,285
2011	Meat packing plants	3831
2013	Sausage & prepared meat products mfrs.	1366
2016	Poultry dressing plants	298
2017	Poultry and egg processors	267
2021	Butter mfrs. - creamery	148
2022	Cheese mfrs. - natural & processed	508
2023	Milk mfrs. - condensed & evaporated	279
2024	Ice Milk & frozen dessert mfrs.	2056
2026	Milk plants - fluid	828
2032	Canned specialties producers	598
2033	Fruit & vegetable canners	721
2034	Fruit, vegetable & soup processors-dehydrated	504
2035	Fruit, vegetable sauces & salad dressing mfrs.	380
2037	Frozen fruit & vegetable mfrs.	316
2038	Frozen specialties mfrs.	581
2041	Flour & other grain mill products plants	397
2043	Cereal breakfast food mfrs.	48
2044	Rice millers	57
2045	Flour mfrs. blended & prepared	116
2046	Corn millers - wet	84
2047	Dog, cat & other pet food mfrs.	215
2048	Feed mfrs. (prepared-animal) n.e.c.	1994
2051	Bread & bakery products mfrs.	1652
2052	Cookie & cracker mfrs.	298
2061	Sugar mfrs. - cane (except refining)	77
2062	Sugar refineries - cane	37
2063	Sugar refineries - beet	45
2065	Candy & confectionery products mfrs.	752
2066	Chocolate & cocoa products mfrs.	91
2067	Gum mfrs. - chewing	14
2074	Cottonseed oil mills	54
2075	Soybean oil mills	81
2076	Vegetable oil mfrs. - ex. corn, cottonseed	63
2077	Oil & fat mfrs. - animal & marine	865
2079	Cooking oil & shortening mfrs.	124
2082	Malt beverage mfrs.	85
2083	Malt mfrs.	32
2084	Wine, brandy & brandy spirits mfrs.	728
2085	Liquor mfrs. - distilled, rectified, blended	95

Fig. 11-1. Food-related manufacturers purchase many products. A list of manufacturers can be an important part of your mail-order business. Choose a list that best represents your ideal market. (Continued.)

S.I.C. Description	*Count for U.S.*
2086 Soft drinks & carbon water mfrs.	.2289
2087 Flavoring extract & syrup mfrs.	.351
2091 Fish & seafood plants - canned & cured	.252
2092 Fish & seafood plants - fresh & frozen	.493
2095 Coffee mfrs. - roasted.	.135
2097 Ice plants - manufactured	.401
2098 Macaroni - Spaghetti mfrs.	.220
2099 Food preparation mfrs. n.e.c.	.1395

Fig. 11-1. Continued.

As you can see, there are many, many lists available to you. The lists are so well developed, many people move into the direct-mail business in hopes of matching their product or service with their target market, and their list becomes the target market. There are lists of accountants, mail-order owners, millionaires, women executives, golf course owners, physics teachers, kindergarten teachers, contributors to charities, and nuclear scientists. You name the group or target market and you or your list broker can find the list.

WHEN DO YOU REMOVE SOMEONE FROM YOUR LIST?

Determining when to remove a name from your list is simple: do it when the person has refused to buy from you for a long period of time. Each list-owner must use a system to keep the list current with people who want to buy. For example, one mail-order owner in California sends out a special 1/2-price offer to everyone on his list—the people who respond and buy remain on his list, the others are removed. Another mail-order owner uses a point system for each customer. Five points are given if the customer purchased during the last year, one point is awarded for each hundred dollars of sales; if a name on the list does not reach 10 points, it is dropped from the list. You must determine when a customer is no longer interested in your offers, and, for the sake of saving time and money, you must take the necessary action.

YOUR LIST HAS A PROFILE

Your house list or the list you rent to mail your offers has a distinct profile, which means that the people on the list have certain characteristics in common. For example, my house list has a profile of my customers which includes the following:

Occupation:	White-collar workers, managers, supervisors, salespeople, business owners.
Income:	Household income: $65,000 to $70,000 yearly

Education:	College Education
Products/services purchased by mail:	Books, newsletters, courses, manuals, seminars, business opportunities.
Age:	30 to 48 years old
Geographic location:	All over the United States

How do you determine this information? You can send a questionnaire to your customers to gather the information, or if you advertise in specific magazines and your inquirers and customers are from these magazines, based on the demographics from the subscriber list, you have a good idea about their profile.

When you rent a list, ask your list broker to give you the profile of the list; this essential information will determine whether or not his list will pull for you. The list broker will get a list data card, which includes the price of the list, the profile of the list, and how the names were obtained, giving the newspaper or magazine used. Figure 11-2 is an example of a data card.

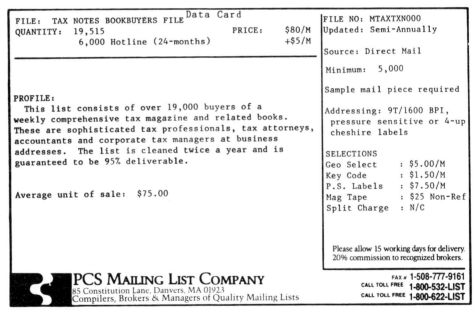

Fig. 11-2. This is similar to the magazine rate card, but includes a profile of the people on the list, price for rental of list, and average unit of sale. Always sample a small portion of a list before renting the whole list.

SHOULD YOU TEST A LIST?

It is an excellent idea to test a small portion of a list to determine whether or not you want to continue to rent it. Testing a list is similar to going to an ice cream shop—before you buy a large cone of ice cream, you can take a small spoon and try some of the flavor you choose. A test of your list can save you time and money. Why send 10,000 or 20,000 offers to names on a list when you might be able to send a test-mailing to 2,000 or 5,000 names on the list. Some list owners will rent a minimum of 5,000 names. When I rent a mailing list, I always request a national cross-section list, which gives me names from all parts of the United States, and this gives me an idea how the list would do all over the country. The size of the list for testing depends on the total number on the list. When I do a small test of 2,000 or 5,000 names, I purchase pressure-sensitive, the peel-and-press labels, so I can put the names right on the envelopes myself when I do the mailing. When your business grows, and you do more direct mailing, you can purchase an address mailing machine to do your mailing for you. Large mail-order dealers turn all their mailing activities over to a letter shop to do it for them.

HOW DO YOU KNOW WHETHER A LIST IS PROFITABLE?

You must make a profit. The profit must be the result of examining your sales from the list and the expenses for the mailing for the list. Let's say you use a rental list of 5,000 names, and you send your sales package to sell your $19.95 manual on building a family room. Let's say you receive a .023 percent response, which is 125 orders for the manual.

Sales		$2,493.75
Expenses		
List Rental	$225.00	
Merchandise Cost	500.00	
Postage	835.00	
Printing/Sales Material	400.00	
Total Cost		$1,960.00
Profit for Mailing		$533.75

You earned $533.75 for that test mailing, and if you mailed out to all the names on the list of 100,000, you would earn 20 times the initial test profits, or $10,675. Notice the cost of the postage is only $835, because this is the special bulk rate the postal service offers to people doing large mailings. The bulk rate saves you over eight cents on the cost of first-class postage. You save $415 on this mailing using the bulk rate. This mailing gives you 125 new customers to sell your other products to in the future. When you mail to all 100,000 names on the rental list, you will increase your house mailing list by 2,000. Remember, you cannot make a copy of the names on your rental list, but once the names on the list respond back to you with an order or a further inquiry, they belong to your own list.

Keying the Name and Address Label   125

"SALTING" THE LIST

The most popular question about mailing lists at my mail-order seminar is how the list owner can tell if his list is being copied. The mailing list owner "salts" the list, which means he uses some names and addresses of people who will keep a list of mail-order offers mailed to them. No purchases are made by them. When they find three or four offers from Jack's Mail-Order Company, and the list owner's records show Jack's company only sent them one order for a test of 5,000, the list owner knows the names were copied. The list owner will not rent to this company again. The list broker is also notified, and once the word gets out in the list rental business that Jack's company plays unfair, it will be difficult for Jack to rent from others in the future. Most list renters also request the list be sent out within a week after delivery to prevent the list from being copied. It is also expensive to copy a 5,000 name list. Why spend the time and money to copy names that might not pull anyway. Don't get involved in copying the names on the list, you may rent your own names out in the future. Play the game the correct way.

BUILD YOUR HOUSE LIST

Make your house list the best possible list. Keep those customers and inquirers happy by sending them your latest offers. Keep it clean. When you get a change in address, correct it right away. Lists, even house lists, age very quickly. Making yours work for you requires close attention to detail.

KEYING THE NAME AND ADDRESS LABEL

The best method to determine which list an order should be credited to is to key the name and address label on the order card. For example, if you used the list of the ABC company for your offer, the name and address label will look like the following:

```
                                              ABC-D

    Ms. Sally Brown
    1 Main Street
    Anytown, MA 01830

```

When you receive this order card with the name and address label above, you can quickly determine if you used the ABC company list. The D signifies you used the $5 discount offer. Make certain that if you are using more than one rental list, you accurately give credit to the correct list.

USE YOUR LIST OF FRIENDS

In this chapter I talked about the importance of a good house list. One of the most important lists is your own list of friends, associates, teachers, classmates, neighbors, colleagues, fellow group members, and people you know personally. This is an important group—these people know you, and trust you, and will be happy to purchase your product or service from you. Don't keep your mail-order business a secret; let the people close to you know about your activities. Put them on your house list. When they respond favorably to you, send them your mailings on a regular basis.

SUMMARY OF KEY POINTS

- Your own house list is valuable. Take care of it, keep it clean, and use it to send your offers to your customers.
- Don't fall into the trap of simply taking names out of a phone book. Your success will depend on your ability to pinpoint the best possible potential customers and tell your complete story. Nothing does this better than a good list.
- Review your house list, mail-response lists, and compiled list to select the best one possible.
- A list broker is your consultant in choosing the best list.
- You usually rent lists rather than buy them.
- Lists age quickly, keep them healthy by keeping your lists clean and classified correctly to get the maximum use from them.
- Use the merge-and-purge system to eliminate duplicate names on various lists.
- Decide whether or not you want to rent your list out for additional money.
- Keep your list secure. It is a valuable resource to you.
- There are hundreds, even thousands, of lists available to rent.
- Remove a name from your list when he or she refuses to buy for an extended period of time.
- Your list has a profile; it includes your customers' incomes, occupations, geographic locations, and lifestyles.
- Test a list before you purchase a large rental order from it.
- Do a profit-and-loss analysis for each list you use.
- Just like a list owner that rents his or her list, salt some names in your list to see if others are using your list without your approval.
- Build your house list into the best list possible.
- Key your lists so you know how to give credit to a list for a sale.

12

Getting Your Mail Out

THE FEELING IS UNBELIEVABLE. YOU HAVE PREPARED AND PRINTED YOUR SALES material and your list is ready. You are ready to do your very first mailing. Your goals are lofty. You want success. You can almost taste it. The one real benefit of direct mail is your opportunity to measure your success or failure quickly. You simply wait a few weeks for the response, and if the response is good, your mailbox is filled with checks and orders. If, on the other hand, after a few weeks the orders dribble in slowly, with few checks and small orders, your spirit is dampened a bit. Your first mailing to your customers is special to you, and I recommend that you do the mailing yourself.

DO IT YOURSELF

Some mail-order owners do their first mailing to get the experience of the various duties involved in a successful mailing. By doing it yourself, you might make a mistake or two, but you will learn from the experience and improve in the future. For example, I recall a student who, on his first bulk mailing, put all his sales letters, reply cards, and reply envelopes into an outside envelope, separated them into various piles, and dropped them off at the local post office. He used the third-class bulk mail rate to save money, instead of sending them out by first class. Since you save money with the bulk rate, you're expected to do the extra sorting by zip codes and states to save the post office time and money. About an hour after he deposited the mail at the counter, he received a call from the post office. They were unhappy with the way he packaged the bulk mail, and they wanted him to come back for the mail. He went back to the post office red-faced, but enthusiastic, and received instructions on the way the post office wanted the mail packaged. He learned the process, and never had a problem again in the future. You'll learn the process by doing it on your own, too.

DO IT RIGHT THE FIRST TIME

If you prepare the mailing correctly, with all pieces properly sorted and sacked, the post office can handle your mail quickly, and it will arrive to the proper destination on time. One way to learn all the regulations of the post office is to use the "bible" of mailing offered by the post office entitled *Domestic Mailing Manual*. You can buy it or order it from your post office.

USING THE THIRD-CLASS BULK RATE

You can file the post office application form #3601 and pay a one-time fee for the permit (Fig. 12-1). You will never have to pay for this permit again, as long as you use it within 12 months. When the post office finds you are not using bulk mail, they can cancel your permit. The other fee is an annual fee for use of the permit for a full 12-month period. If you decide to use the third-class bulk rate method of mailing, use it regularly.

The postal service defines third-class bulk mail as including pieces that weigh less than 16 ounces, are not required to be mailed at the first-class rate (i.e., they don't include any handwritten or typewritten material), and are not entered as second-class mail. Third-class mailing can be used when each mailing is of at least 200 pieces or weighs 50 or more pounds. All pieces must be of the same processing category, such as letters, flats, or catalogs. Many of my students in my seminars on mail order like the idea of the bulk rate, but are surprised when they learn that all mailing pieces must be identical in size, and at least 200 pieces.

The real benefit of the third-class bulk mail rate is the money you save. For example, if you send out 200 pieces by bulk rate, you will save almost $.09 on each piece or $18.00 for the total mailing. Check with your post office for rates—the rates change periodically. The mail might not move as fast as when you send the mail by first-class mail, but your bulk mail will move across the country within a week to a week and a half.

```
                              U.S. POSTAL SERVICE
              APPLICATION TO MAIL WITHOUT AFFIXING POSTAGE STAMPS
```

APPLICANT: File at office where mailings will be made with required fee.

NAME OF APPLICANT *(Print or type)*   APPLICANT'S TELEPHONE NO.

ADDRESS OF APPLICANT *(Street, Apt./Suite No., City, State and ZIP Code) (Print or Type)*

AVERAGE NUMBER OF PIECES IN EACH MAILING | CLASS OF MAIL MATTER | SIGNATURE OF APPLICANT | DATE

CLASS OF MAIL MATTER:
☐ FIRST   ☐ SECOND
☐ THIRD   ☐ FOURTH

TO BE COMPLETED BY POSTMASTER ▶ | AMOUNT OF FEE COLLECTED $ | PERMIT NUMBER | DATE OF ISSUANCE

POSTMASTER: Retain application in your file. When approved, deliver authorization to permit holder.

PS Form 3601, July 1980

```
                              U.S. POSTAL SERVICE
              AUTHORIZATION TO MAIL WITHOUT AFFIXING POSTAGE STAMPS
```

You are authorized to mail at this post office matter bearing permit imprints, postage to be paid in money.

POST OFFICE *(City, State and ZIP Code)*

PERMIT NUMBER | DATE OF ISSUANCE | SIGNATURE OF POSTMASTER

NAME OF PERMIT HOLDER *(Address, Apt./Suite No., City, State and ZIP Code)*

TO:

PS Form July 1980 3601   ☆ U.S. GOVERNMENT PRINTING OFFICE: 1984— 754-006/10202

Fig. 12-1. Form #3601 can be obtained at your local post office. It must be completed and returned with required fees at the post office where you plan to do your mailing. This gives your permission to mail without affixing postage stamps, and permission can be canceled when you fail to use it within 12 months.

HOW DO YOU PREPARE BULK-RATE MAILING?

The post office requires that you package the pieces so the postal service can process the mail faster. The post office will supply you with rubberbands and stickers so you can process your mailing. The post office requires you to follow certain steps to earn the special bulk rate. Figure 12-2 lists the requirements for packaging bulk third-class mail. Figure 12-3 shows how to label your bulk mail packages properly.

FIRST-CLASS MAIL

First-class mail is the fastest way to ship your mail, but because of the speed and priority given to it, it will be more expensive. There are fewer restrictions, and

Bulk Third-Class Basic Rate Packaging Requirements

STEP 1—MAKE 5-DIGIT PACKAGES

You are required to:

A.   Sort 10 or more pieces with same 5-digit zip code into 5-digit packages.

B.   Label with red (D) or no label in lower left-hand corner of top piece.

C.   Prepare packages 4″ thick or smaller and use two thick rubberbands.

D.   Exhaust all possibilities of making this type package before going to step 2.

STEP 2—MAKE 3-DIGIT PACKAGES

You are required to:

A.   Sort 10 or more pieces with same 3-digit zip code into 3-digit packages.

B.   Label with green (3) in lower left-hand corner of top piece.

C.   Prepare packages 4″ thick or smaller and use two thick rubberbands.

D.   Exhaust all possibilities of making this type package before going to step 3.

STEP 3—MAKE (same) STATE PACKAGES

You are required to:

A.   Sort 10 or more pieces with same state into state packages.

B.   Label with orange (S) in lower left-hand corner of top piece.

C.   Make packages 4″ thick or smaller and use two thick rubberbands.

D.   Exhaust all possibilities of making this type package before going to step 4.

STEP 4—MAKE (mixed) STATES PACKAGES

You are required to:

A.   Sort all remaining pieces into a mixed states package.

B.   Label with a facing slip. A facing slip is a 3″ or 4″ slip of paper with the words ''Mixed States'' boldly printed on it. Put the facing slip underneath the two thick or smaller.

Fig. 12-2. You save money on bulk mail because you prepare the mail for easy handling by the post office. There are four different packages: digit packages, 3-digit packages, state packages, and mixed states packages.

the mail will be forwarded to sender if a forwarding address is available at the post office. I suggest you use first-class mail to send out your responses to inquiries from your magazine advertisements. You should also send out your bills using first-class postage. Some mail-order owners use first-class postage for their first small mailing because of the speed of delivery, and they get a response right away. The first-class mail will be returned to you if it cannot be delivered.

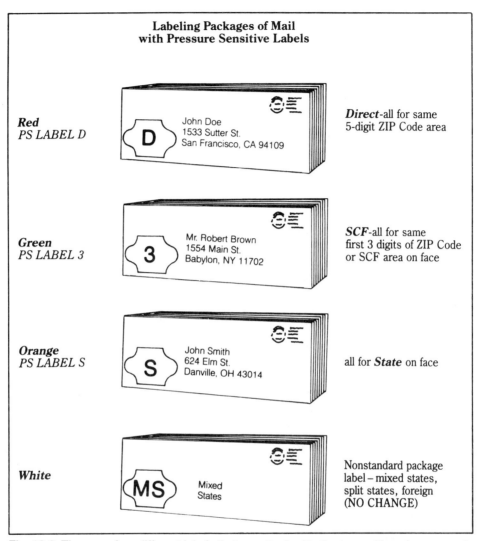

**Labeling Packages of Mail
with Pressure Sensitive Labels**

Red
PS LABEL D

D

John Doe
1533 Sutter St.
San Francisco, CA 94109

Direct-all for same
5-digit ZIP Code area

Green
PS LABEL 3

3

Mr. Robert Brown
1554 Main St.
Babylon, NY 11702

SCF-all for same
first 3 digits of ZIP Code
or SCF area on face

Orange
PS LABEL S

S

John Smith
624 Elm St.
Danville, OH 43014

all for **State** on face

White

MS

Mixed
States

Nonstandard package
label – mixed states,
split states, foreign
(NO CHANGE)

Fig. 12-3. There are four different labels that are attached to the top mailing piece on each mailing package. These labels are available free at the post office where you do your mailing. Keep a sufficient supply on hand.

FIRST-CLASS PRESORT SPECIAL RATE

If you send at least 500 pieces of first-class mail, all identical in weight and size, the post office will give you a special rate. You must be willing to do the necessary sorting of the pieces and also pay a yearly fee, as well as a one-time first-class permit fee. This presort rate is very favorable for companies requiring large weekly or monthly mailings where speed is required. Some mailers save almost $.04 on each piece mailed using the presort rate.

SECOND-CLASS MAIL

This class of mail is devoted to magazines, societies, and associations, which regularly publish periodicals and newspapers. A second-class mailing permit gives them an excellent rate for their mailings. Most mail-order companies cannot use the second-class permit to mail their sales materials.

CONTROLLED CIRCULATION PUBLICATIONS

The post office can accept certain direct-mail advertising as a controlled circulation publication. The publication cannot be owned by an individual or business concern, and it cannot be used as an auxiliary to advance or increase the business.

SPECIAL NONPROFIT THIRD-CLASS

This is a special class offered by the postal service for nonprofit organizations. To become authorized for this special rate, you must submit a post office form #3624, with supporting documents. Not all nonprofit organizations qualify for this special rate. The most common are nonprofit religious, educational, scientific, philanthropic, agricultural, labor-related, veteran-related, and fraternal organizations. This special permit cannot be transferred to another organization. None of the income of the organization can involve any private stockholder or individual, and the name of the nonprofit organization must be clearly displayed on the outside of the mailing.

HOW DO YOU PAY FOR BULK RATE?

Your postage can be paid by check at the post office when you deliver your bulk mailing. When you use the permit imprint, whereby you print your permit number on the outside of your envelope, you will save a great deal of time and money. You also have the option of using meter stamps, precancelled stamps, or envelopes, all supplied by the post office. A mailing statement must be completed for both the imprint mailing, and the meter stamps mailing. See Fig. 12-4 for postal service form #3602 for the imprint mailing, and Fig. 12-5 for form #3602-PC for the meter stamps mailing. Both of these forms are available free from your local post office. If you find your local post office has run out of these forms, they will order them for you, free of charge. Take a supply and use when needed.

When you need assistance, call the bulk-rate mail department of your post office. They will be more than happy to help you put your mailing out successfully. Once you get the bulk mailing together, bring it to the post office. Use the right forms, methods, and techniques to save yourself time and money.

PS Form 3602, July 1988 | FOR ZONE RATED MAIL USE FORM 3605 | Side A

| U.S. Postal Service **STATEMENT OF MAILING WITH PERMIT IMPRINTS** | MAILER: Complete all items by typewriter, pen or indelible pencil. Prepare in duplicate if receipt is desired. Check for instructions from your postmaster regarding box labeled "RCA Offices." | Permit No. |

| Post Office of Mailing | Date | Receipt No. | Fed. Agency Subcode | Mailing Statement Sequence No. |

Check applicable box

1st Class
- [ ] International
- [ ] ZIP+4 Nonpresort
- [ ] ZIP+4 Presort
  - [ ] DMM 365 Mailing
  - [ ] DMM 366 Mailing

1st Class
- [ ] ZIP+4 Barcoded
- [ ] Carrier Route
- [ ] Presort First-Class
- [ ] Single Piece
- [ ] Other (Specify)

Processing Category (See DMM 128)
- [ ] Letters
- [ ] Flats
- [ ] Machinable Parcels
- [ ] Irregular Parcels
- [ ] Outside Parcels

Weight of a single piece: __ . __ __ __ __ lbs.

Mailing Identification Code:

TOTAL IN MAILING / **NUMBER OF**

Pieces	Pounds	Sacks	Trays	Pallets	Other Containers

Name and Address of Permit Holder (Include ZIP Code) | Telephone No.

POSTAGE COMPUTATION

Name and Address of Individual or Organization for which mailing is prepared (If other than permit holder)

Name and Address of Mailing Agent (If other than permit holder)

Piece Rates

		No. Qual. Pieces	Rate Per Piece $	Postage
1.	ZIP+4 Barcoded			
2.	ZIP+4 Presort			
3.	Presort First Class			
4.	ZIP+4 Nonpresort			
5.	Carrier Route			
6.	Rate Category	No. of Pieces	Rate Per Piece $	
7.	SUBTOTAL (1 through 6) ▶			Postage

8. Additional Postage Payment (State reasons for additional postage payment under "Comments" below) | No. of Pieces | Rate/Piece $ | Postage

9. **TOTAL POSTAGE** (7 plus 8) where applicable ────────▶ | Total Postage $

The submission of a false, fictitious or fraudulent statement may result in imprisonment of up to 5 years and a fine of up to $10,000. (18 U.S.C. 1001) In addition, a civil penalty of up to $5,000 and an additional assessment of twice the amount falsely claimed may be imposed. (31 U.S.C. 3802)

I hereby certify that all information furnished on this form is accurate and truthful, and that this material presented qualifies for the rates of postage claimed.

Signature of Permit Holder or Agent (Both principal and agent are liable for any postage deficiency incurred) | Telephone No.

I CERTIFY that this mailing has been inspected to verify that it qualifies for the rate of postage being paid, and that it is properly prepared (and presorted where required) and that the statement of mailing has been verified and the necessary annual fee has been paid. | Round Stamp (Required)

Signature of Weigher | Time | A.M. | P.M.

Comments:

PS Form **3602**, July 1988 | FINANCIAL DOCUMENT – FORWARD TO FINANCE OFFICE

Fig. 12-4. Form #3602 is red in color and used when you have your permit on your mailing of over 200 pieces. You can write a check payable to your post office on the day of your mailing.

PS Form **3602-PC**, Apr. 1985   **FOR ZONE RATED MAIL USE FORM 3605**

| U.S. Postal Service **STATEMENT OF MAILING BULK RATES** | **MAILER:** Complete all items by typewriter, pen or indelible pencil. Prepare in duplicate if receipt is desired. Check for instructions from your postmaster regarding box labeled "RCA Offices." | **Permit No.** |

Post Office of Mailing	Date	Receipt No.	Mailing Statement Sequence No.

Check applicable box

- ☐ *International*

1st Class
- ☐ *ZIP + 4 Nonpresort*
- ☐ *ZIP + 4 Presort*
- ☐ *Carrier Route*
- ☐ *Presort First-Class*
- ☐ *Single Piece*

2nd Class
- ☐ *Newspapers and magazines entered at the applicable third-class rate*

3rd Class
- ☐ *Carrier Route*
- ☐ *5-digit*
- ☐ *Basic*
- ☐ *Single Piece*

4th Class
- ☐ *Library Rate*
- ☐ *Special 4th Class Single Pie*
- ☐ *Presort Special 4th Class*

- ☐ *Other (Specify)*

Postage is being paid by: *(Check one)*   ☐ Pre Canceled Stamps   ☐ Meter Stamps

Processing Category *(See DMM 128)*
- ☐ *Letters*
- ☐ *Flats*
- ☐ *Machinable Parcels*
- ☐ *Irregular Parcels*
- ☐ *Outside Parcels*

Weight of a single piece — — — — — lbs.   **RCA Offices:**

TOTAL IN MAILING   **NUMBER OF**

Pieces	Pounds	Sacks	Trays	Pallets	Other Containers

Name and Address of Permit Holder *(Include ZIP Code)*	Telephone No.

POSTAGE COMPUTATION

Pound Rate	1. Pound Rate Postage Charge	No. Pounds	Rate/Pound $	Postage
Piece Rates	2. ZIP + 4 Presort	No. Qual. Pieces	Rate Per Piece $	Postage
	3. Presort First Class	No. Qual. Pieces	Rate Per Piece $	Postage
	4. ZIP + 4 Nonpresort	No Qual. Pieces	Rate Per Piece $	Postage
	5. Carrier Route	No. Qual. Pieces	Rate Per Piece $	Postage
	6. 5-digit	No. Qual. Pieces	Rate Per Piece $	Postage
	7. Basic	No. Qual. Pieces	Rate Per Piece $	Postage
	8. Rate Category	No. of Pieces	Rate Per Piece $	Postage
	9. **SUBTOTAL (1 through 8)** ▶			Postage

☐ Check if non-profit under 623. DMM*

Name and Address of Individual or Organization for which mailing is prepared *(If other than permit holder)*

☐ Check if non-profit under 623. DMM*

Name and Address of Mailing Agent *(If other than permit holder)*

10. Additional Postage Payment *(State reasons for additional postage payments)*	No. of Pieces	Rate/Piece $	Postage

11. ☐ Check if applicable third class bulk pound rate is paid by permit imprint. *(Form 3602 required)*

12. TOTAL POSTAGE *(9 plus 10)* where applicable ━━━━━▶ | Total Postage $

* The signature of a nonprofit mailer certifies that: (1) The mailing does not violate section 623.5 DMM; and (2) Only the mailer's matter is being mailed; and (3) This is not a cooperative mailing with other persons or organizations that are not entitled to special bulk mailing privileges; and (4) This mailing has not been undertaken by the mailer on behalf of or produced for another person or organization that is not entitled to special bulk mailing privileges.

Willful entry of false, fictitious or fraudulent statements or representations hereon, punishable by fine up to $10,000 or imprisonment up to 5 years, or both (18 USC 1001).

Signature of Permit Holder or Agent *(Both principal and agent are liable for any postage deficiency incurred)*   Telephone No.

Round Stamp (Required)

I CERTIFY that this mailing has been inspected to verify that it qualifies for the rate of postage being paid, and that it is properly prepared (and presorted where required) and that the statement of mailing has been verified and the necessary annual fee has been paid

Signature of Weigher	Time	A.M. / P.M.

PS Form **3602-PC**, Apr. 1985   ✿ U.S. GPO: 1985—477-096/39209   **FINANCIAL DOCUMENT – FORWARD TO FINANCE OFFICE**

Fig. 12-5. Form #3602-PC is green in color and used by the mailer when using meter-stamp mailing. Fill out the form by typewriter, pen, or indelible pencil. The post office will accept a check for the mailing.

FOURTH-CLASS MAIL

The fourth-class rate includes the library rate, special fourth-class rate for books and manuscripts, and the presort special fourth-class rate. The special rate for books is very important for mail-order owners selling books and manuals. Check with your post office to see if you can use the fourth-class rate.

FIRST-CLASS PERMIT

A first-class permit is issued to you by the post office and permits you to print this information on your reply envelope, so your customers can mail their own order to you without using a stamp. Some mail-order owners find that this permit increases their returns—a customer would put his reply into the mail quickly, rather than search around for stamps to send the order. You must pay a fee to receive this permit, and the post office will charge you a fee for all mail returned to you. Expect some prospects to send you little notes without their orders—you are still required to pay for them. Most reply envelopes are filled with an order and payment. Figure 12-6 shows a reply envelope with a first-class permit.

Do you need a first-class permit? Some mail-order companies use the first-class permit because it makes their mailing package look official, and they make an extra effort to inform the prospects that no stamp is needed to order.

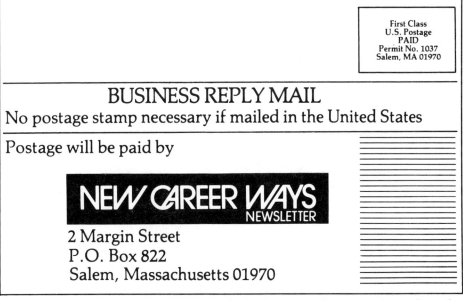

Fig. 12-6. The first-class permit envelope permits the potential customer to send you the order without attaching a stamp. Some potential customers abuse this by sending notes and other messages without ordering.

POST OFFICE SEMINARS

Periodically, the post office, usually a regional post office, will run seminars on how a business such as yours can use the services of the post office. At the seminar they will give you rates, forms, and free supplies such as stickers and rubber bands for the bulk mailings. Call your post office to find out when the next seminar will be presented. The post office can offer helpful advice and ideas to save you both time and money.

OTHER DELIVERY SERVICES

To send mailings, the post office can give you the best price and service. For shipments of products to customers, you might consider many other small-package freight carriers. These independent carriers are competitive in price for packages, but they cannot deliver to post office boxes—they can only ship to street addresses. Some mail-order people are very happy with their services and the ability to trace a package if there is a delivery problem. Consider the independent carrier for your package deliveries.

DO YOU NEED A POST OFFICE BOX?

The post office rents out various sizes of mailboxes and will give you your own key, so you can pick up your mail at your convenience. This prevents your business mail from getting mixed with your personal mail. Usually the post office rents out the boxes for three months at a time. Some mail-order owners use both their street address and their post office number to make certain the mail is delivered correctly. Others use their street and number to add credibility to their business, as some customers get nervous when they mail their order to a post office box.

To get a post office box, you might have to put your name on a waiting list, if the post office has no more available boxes. In the meantime, you can rent a mailbox at an independent mailbox business in your area. These businesses not only rent mailboxes, they ship packages, make copies, sell money orders, and perform numerous other important services for the small-business person.

The real benefit of using a rental mailbox, either from the post office or a commercial mailing company, is that you can check your mail two or three times a week, gather all the mail and act on each one, and the job is completed. On the other hand, when you get mail at home, mixed in with personal mail, it will take additional time and effort to process the mail. Set a goal to build your business so large you will need a large box at the post office to handle your checks, orders, and materials. Set a goal that your business will expand so large that the post office personnel will know your company because of the volume of your mail.

USING LETTER SHOPS

Once your business grows, you might consider using letter shop services who perform partial or complete mailing services. For example, you might only want the letter shop to insert your sales letters, brochures, and order cards into the envelopes. Or you might want the letter shop to do your third-class bulk mailing for you. Some letter shops are completely automated, while others are smaller with limited machinery. Some letter shops also handle your mailing list for you. Some mail-order owners spend too much time on duties that could be assigned to a letter shop.

Visit the letter shop and ask for a presentation of their facilities. Be sure to get a full understanding of the services they can provide to you. Give the letter shop a small job in the beginning to see the quality of their work and compare it with the cost. Is the value on the same level as the cost? Is the value higher than the cost? Make certain of the services you want completed and the cost for these services before ordering them. Get your contract in writing, clearly spelling out the work you want completed and the cost. Give the letter shop sufficient time to complete the job. When you try to rush a job, mistakes—sometimes costly ones—can happen.

MAILING CAN INCREASE YOUR HOUSE LIST

Nothing builds a successful mail-order business better than continuous mailing and turning inquiries into customers. Your customers enjoy receiving new offers from you. They enjoy hearing from you. Regular mailings show you want their business, and you have new offers to share with them. Keep building and mailing out to your house list. This will become your harvest of the future.

HANDLE INQUIRIES DAILY

Some of my mail-order students confuse mailings with handling inquiries. A mailing is when you send an offer to a specific list, handling inquiries means you send out mail daily to those people who responded to your magazine advertisement. Treat each inquiry with kid gloves, and lay the groundwork for a lasting friendship. By getting into the practice of handling the inquiries daily, you lay the foundation to build a long relationship with the customer. Act today, but make certain to include all the information the customer needs to make his decision. When you cannot include all the information he or she needs, tell the customer the reason why, and then deliver the additional information as soon as possible. Now let's summarize this chapter.

SUMMARY OF KEY POINTS

- Do the mailing yourself. By doing the mailing yourself you will gain important information about the mailing process, especially how to use the bulk-rate mailing method.
- Know the advantages and disadvantages of first-class rates, first-class presort special rates, second-class rates, and controlled circulation rates.
- Use the best mailing class for the needs of your business.
- Permit the postal service to be a partner in your business.
- Follow each step carefully in the bulk-rate mailing process. If done incorrectly, it will delay your mailing.
- One advantage to using the bulk rate is the single check payment for the mailing.
- Learn how to complete the statement of mailing with permit imprints, and the statement of mailing bulk rates. Some mailers can use the fourth-class mail rate.
- The first-class permit is used to permit your customers to send their orders without using postage stamps. You might find that the first-class permit can increase your returns.
- The post office frequently offers free seminars—take advantage of them.
- You can use other commercial shippers to deliver your products or services.
- Consider renting a mailbox at the post office.
- You have the option of using a letter shop to do your mailings once your business is established.
- The real value of the regular mailing is the opportunity to build up your house list. Keep your inquirers happy by mailing their requests daily.

13

Keep Your Customers Buying

MAIL-ORDER BUSINESSES ARE BUILT ON SELLING YOUR CUSTOMER OVER AND over again. Your ability to resell your customer will make the difference between an average mail-order business and one that succeeds for the big time. This chapter will give you ideas about how to build that winning relationship with your customer. One mail-order owner in Minnesota keeps his business going strong by sending regular mailing offering new products and informing the customers of his commitment to offer top value, great service, and quality products. Successful mail-order owners continue to give their customers new ideas and better offers to keep them buying.

WHAT IS A TYPICAL DAY FOR YOUR CUSTOMER?

Successful mail-order owners know their customers. They understand (or at least make an effort to understand) the process of the customers mentally visualizing the product, deciding if they want it, and then acting on their decision. Once, in order to get a clearer picture of my market I interviewed one of my customers. I found that her average day consisted of getting up at 6 A.M. each morning to prepare for a full day's work, commuting to Boston, working in a large insurance company, dealing with difficult people in the claims department, and returning home at 6 P.M. I learned that my customer reviews her mail each

139

evening, which, on a typical day, includes around 26 pieces. My customer lives in an affluent suburb of Boston, and this partially accounts for the excessive mail volume (many mailers select high-income geographical locations). Of the 26 pieces, 10 are first class, 5 are catalogs, and 11 are direct-mail pieces offering various products and services. The direct-mail pieces vary from selling time-share property to magazine subscriptions. My typical customer reads two of the five catalogs sent to her. Many of the direct-mail pieces are left unread, some are left unopened. Since this practice is representative of the average customer, your biggest challenge is finding a method to get your customers and prospects to open your mailings, and then act on them with an order.

OFFER INFORMATION

A successful mail-order owner in California found himself answering many letters from customers asking about ways to run their businesses. The owner decided to start a newsletter offering advice to his customers. The newsletter was short and to the point, and at the end of the newsletter, offered the customers a well-presented listing of his products. Presenting important information together with offers is an excellent way to be of service to your customers and increase your profits.

REGULAR MAILINGS KEEP YOUR CUSTOMERS INTERESTED

You spent a good amount of money to get your customers, and the only way you can continue to keep them as customers is to keep the communication process going. If your customer does not hear from you for months, he or she might start buying from your competitor, and then it is even more difficult to keep the customer. Please use the "Mailings" worksheet in Fig. 13-1 to keep track of your mailings. Keep your customer on your side by regular mailings offering the latest developments in your specific mail-order field.

OFFER SPECIAL DISCOUNTS TO CUSTOMERS

Customers enjoy an incentive, such as a 10 percent off coupon when the purchase is made within 10 days. One mail-order owner in Illinois sent his customers a free newsletter when they ordered at least $50 in products or services. Other mail-order companies use the rebate strategy: they send a $5 rebate in the mailing to give their customer a further incentive to buy their products. Ask yourself what is the best incentive possible to motivate your customer to buy from you. Try to avoid giving away too much, and keep the focus on the quality and uniqueness of your products and services. Remember, these special customers are not buying your discounts; they are buying all the services your company offers them. Your job is to serve them better.

mailings

WEEK _____

DATE	PROPOSITION	MAILING	LIST	TOTAL

Fig. 13-1. This worksheet can keep you current on the amount of mailings and the dates sent, along with the specific markets, list used, and the proposition.

SEND A QUESTIONNAIRE

Your mail-order customers can give you valuable information on themselves, their goals, their problems, and their need for products or services. Many customers enjoy offering their opinions, needs, and wants to interested parties. You are special to them because they purchased from you in the past and they trust and respect you. They feel you are deserving of their information and, in turn, will be happy to answer your questionnaire. In addition, the information on the questionnaire will turn the names and addresses into real people with needs and wants. Your challenge will be to develop follow-up mailings and creative incentives to keep them buying from you.

TELL OTHERS ABOUT YOUR PRODUCTS OR SERVICES

Just because you sell your products and services by mail does not prevent you from telling others in-person about your business. Don't hide your business behind your desk. For example, Alice W. sells business products by mail; she has her own office at home and has built the business steadily during the last six months. One day, while she was working at home the phone rang. The president of a local professional club asked Alice to speak to their group at a future meeting. Alice almost declined the invitation, but then she realized this was a golden opportunity to tell potential customers about herself, her business, and how her products and services could help the members of the club. Alice accepted the invitation, and with a little practice and preparation, gave an excellent talk and opened up new sales and customers. The talk focused on how the correct business products can improve profits for business people. I talked to Alice recently, and she told me another club called her and asked her to appear at their club for another talk. Get excited about your business, product, and service, and you will find business coming from all directions.

RUN A SEMINAR

People want information and will pay for it. A successful mail-order owner in California has developed an excellent reputation as a consultant on the marketing, distribution, and promotion of specialized books. He offers seminars in California and in various parts of the country, in order to stay in touch with his customers. At the seminars, he offers various books and lists to his customers. In your own business, you should consider a morning or afternoon seminar for the customers who live in your area. This would allow you to meet them face-to-face and get an even better opportunity to serve them.

What price would you charge for the seminar? Excellent question. You should charge a *fair* price. Some mail-order owners charge just enough to cover their costs, others charge enough to make a profit for their time. For example, one mail-order owner ran a seminar on wooden children's toys to find new dealers, and charged only $25 to cover his costs for the two-hour seminar. The seminar was held in a function room of a large hotel in his local area. Another mail-order dealer ran an excellent seminar and charged $69. Keeping costs as low as possible and charging a fair price will help you to do a winning seminar.

SELL YOUR PRODUCTS OR SERVICES TO AN ASSOCIATION

A mail-order owner from Florida who sells printing supplies increased his business by selling his products to fellow members of a small-business association in his area. The mail-order owner sent out material showing how the businessperson can purchase printing supplies in large quantities and save. Selling to a fellow member of an organization gives you an edge because you have something in common with the member. Some mail-order owners advertise their products and services in the association newsletter mailed monthly to all members. The best way to determine whether or not you can sell your association members is to talk with the president of the organization and ask about it. When the president gives you the approval, you might even ask about renting the mailing list of the organization for your own mailing.

MAIL TO SPECIFIC GEOGRAPHIC AREAS

Mail your offers to the areas of the country or of your state that are buying your products or services. For example, one large sporting and hunting mail-order company mails to one specific town in Massachusetts. This specific town is unique. It has the highest income of any other city or town in the state. Because of this high income, the mail-order business will send their catalog to every household in the town. Their results are excellent, and they continue this practice year after year. It will be up to you to present your offers to the best possible prospects.

USE SAMPLES TO HELP YOU SELL

Nothing sells better than a sample of your own product or service. Give your prospects a chance to see your product, feel it, and use it, so they can get a better understanding about your product. Al LaPoint, a mail-order owner in Massachusetts, sends a 2-inch-square swatch of material to help him sell his high-quality industrial rainsuits to construction companies. A free catalog is sent with a personal letter to all first-time buyers. Al is building his house list to over 2,000 customers.

USE THE CALENDAR

Having a mail-order strategy means doing a mailing with the time of year in mind. The two months preceding Christmas is an excellent time to focus on how your product or service can be a holiday gift. Many mail-order companies do a special mailing just for the Christmas season buyers. A Rhode Island mail-order company sells stocking stuffers by mail as a service to their customers who were found in the past to buy stocking stuffers from various stores.

Keep your eye on the calendar and feature spring and summer products and services during January and February. The spring and summer seasons will require you to sell products for use in the fall and winter. Just as a retail clothing store continues to change their clothes according to the season, you must also continue to display products and services for the future. Sell all year long, not just for one time of year.

REVIEW YOUR PROMISES

What promises are you offering in your advertisements? Do you promise too much? Do you promise too little? Do you focus enough on the benefits of your product? Some mail-order companies just present their product and expect the prospect to buy it. Go over the copy in your sales package periodically to determine if the promises are strong enough to generate a sale. Ask yourself whether or not you would buy the product if this sales package arrived in your mailbox. Talk about benefits—the important reasons the customer should buy from you.

KEEP YOUR FOCUS CONSISTENT

Many mail-order businesses run into trouble when they change their focus in their business. For example, if you want to sell tools, do not change to children's toys. Focus on tools, and make your business better by selecting the best possible products and offering them to the best possible prospects. Too often mail-order owners get discouraged with their product line and switch to something else. Their customers and prospects become confused and they may buy from your competitor. Keep your original strategy by being consistent, so your market will get to know you, trust you, and buy from you.

REVIEW YOUR PROSPECTS

Your sales volume not only reflects on your product or service, it reflects your advertising program as well. Review the magazines you are presently using to gather inquiries. Which advertisements are pulling the most inquiries? What inquiries are turning into sales? Why continue advertising with a magazine that is not working for you? Change to another magazine to reach new prospects with the purchasing power to buy from you. Perhaps you need to add new products designed for women. Perhaps more teenage customers are needed. Perhaps you need to advertise in more publications. The more advertisements you place, the higher the inquiries, and when the inquiries are good ones, your sales will increase.

COMBINE INQUIRIES AND DIRECT-MAIL MAILING

Be creative in the way you manage your business. Keep sending out your packages for inquiries, and periodically—say, each month—send a mailing to your inquirers or customers. Keep your name, product, or service in front of your prospective customers with regular advertising and mailing.

DO NOT FOOL YOUR PROSPECTS

A mail-order owner from New York recently ran an advertisement with a promise to send free information on little-known home businesses to earn exceptionally good income. I was curious, so I sent a postcard to request the information. The information was a two-page sales letter, a short brochure, an inexpensive reply card, and a reply envelope with information on stuffing envelopes at home. I did not read the information. I simply threw it out. The offer promised more than the owner could deliver. In your business make an effort to send them information that will match your customer's expectations. For example, if you promise to send them information on rings and watches, send them information on these items, not on modern art. You will add credibility when you send your inquirers what they expected from your advertisement.

WRITE A SMALL ARTICLE FOR A PUBLICATION

Some mail-order owners write articles about their business, their hobby, or an interest, and publish it in a related magazine. For example, I wrote an article on time management for a mail-order magazine, and instead of being paid for the article, I received a free advertisement in the magazine. The readers of the magazine read my article and this exposure increased the response to my advertisement. The key point is that you develop a reputation for knowledge about a particular field, and people will seek you out to inquire about your product and service.

What can you write about? Write something you know a good deal about. It is always easier to write about something you have first-hand knowledge of, or a great deal of interest in, than something you read about in a book or magazine. Write about your key strengths. For example, a mail-order owner from Michigan, sells cartoons to various publications, and he recently wrote an article on how cartoons can increase readership of an article. The article was well received because the writer knew the subject.

TELL THEM YOU CARE

Show concern when your customers fail to order from you. Ask them why they did not respond to the last mailing. Show them there is a sense of urgency in your business. You want to please them. You want them to stay in contact with you by purchasing your product or service. One mail-order owner from Mississippi includes a small sheet of paper on his second or third mailing to his former customer:

> Dear Mary Brown,
>
> I haven't heard from you!
>
> I sent you my spring and fall mailings of our new offers, but to no avail.
>
> Please take a moment to fill out the enclosed order card, and I will send your order immediately.
>
> Let me know if there is anything I can do for you. A satisfied customer is important to our success.
>
> Thanks,
Lucy

A small reminder to your customer is one method to show him or her you keep track of your orders and the customers who fail to order your products. Your customer is more apt to review your proposal again, and order from you. Sooner or later, you must make the hard decision to remove those customers and inquirers who fail to order from you for an extended period of time.

SELL TO DEALERS

You can sell more products when you sell to other dealers. These dealers own mailing lists of satisfied customers. Dealers are individual business people, just like yourself, and are willing to purchase a product if they can make a profit from it. Dealers can be store owners or they can be mail-order dealers who sell by distributing their catalog. Dealers have their own unique ways to sell their products and can be very helpful for beginning mail-order owners.

One mail-order owner from Maine sells cassette tapes to retailers, and with the help of a specialized mailing list, he is now selling his product all over the country. The specialized mailing list gives him retail stores that purchase his products. A copy of the brochure he uses is shown in Fig. 13-2.

Your copy for dealers must be different than for the average customer. The dealer wants you to discuss margins, costs, benefits, and how this product or service will increase their profits. The dealer wants to know the discount given and the suggested retail price. The dealer might also appreciate a sample product so he or she can take a closer look at the product to see if they can sell it

Look What 4½ Inches of Counter Space Can Do For You!

CASSETTES ONLY 4^{99}
ALL THE GREATEST HITS!

Earn An Extra $100 - $200 Per Month!

How is this possible? By adding our GREATEST HITS TAPE PROGRAM to increase your store's profits.

The program features "AEROSMITH", "JIM CROCE", "ELVIS", "THE BEATLES", "CHUCK BERRY", "ALABAMA", "ELTON JOHN", "ERIC CLAPTON", "STEVE MILLER" and many more!

The 7 MONEY-MAKING FEATURES of our GREATEST HITS TAPE PROGRAM include:

- 1. PROVEN merchandising program designed for convenience stores.
- 2. Pre-selected BEST SELLING Tapes.
- 3. GUARANTEED Sales and Profits.
- 4. FREE SHIPPING for minimum order.
- 5. PROFESSIONAL service.
- 6. Our experience shows this program is the HIGHEST PROFIT MAKER on your counter.
- 7. YOU ARE IMPORTANT TO US. We work hard to help you win more profits.

SPECIAL INTRODUCTORY OFFER:
We will send you a FREE SAMPLE TAPE when you request more information on this GREATEST HITS TAPE PROGRAM.

Here's your next step: Today — fill out the enclosed POSTCARD for more profitable information. Or simply call us and receive your FREE SAMPLE TAPE.
207-439-4911

Maxam Music
Distributors
69 Dennett Road
Kittery, Maine
207-439-4911

Fig. 13-2. A brochure works closely with the sales letter to show the important parts of the product, or details little-known features and benefits of the product or service. The brochure gives important information to the potential buyer to help you get the sale.

successfully. The dealer is also interested in the shipping costs, and what advertising or marketing strategy is the best possible one to use in selling your product or service.

HOW DO YOU REACH THE DEALERS?

You can reach mail-order dealers by using mail-order magazines. You can reach retail stores with specialized magazines. You might want to use a small classified advertisement to generate inquiries and then follow up with more information to describe your product or service. Another approach is to do a mailing of dealers by renting a list or using a directory. One mail-order owner sells sunglasses and sends regular mailings to some resort dealers. One large order from a dealer will increase your sales substantially. Many mail-order businesses gain profits and exposure by selling to dealers.

USE THAT TELEPHONE

Many mail-order owners concentrate primarily on advertising and their mailing package, and give little if any consideration to the telephone. The telephone is an essential part of the buying process. Many of my customers call with a question about my product before they buy it. When I answer the question satisfactorily, they buy it. Do you put your telephone number on your mail-order sales letter? When the customer sees your name and telephone number on your letter, it adds credibility to your offer. You might even request that your customer call you collect to make the offer to communicate to that important customer. Don't make the mistake of hiding behind a post-office box number, without the telephone number in your mailing package.

STAY ON GOOD TERMS WITH YOUR SUPPLIER

Your supplier of your mail-order product or service is not only important to you, but essential to your success. Keep your account paid so you can receive prompt shipments to keep your shipments to your own customers up-to-date. Your supplier can keep you current on changes in the field and aware of new products available. Ask your supplier to send you the latest offers, catalogs, and listing.

HANDLE IRATE CUSTOMERS CAREFULLY

Just because you do not see your customer's face does not mean you will avoid the irate customer. The mail-order complainer may take the time to write their complaint on a sheet of paper, or call you on the phone. You must take this complaint as seriously as you would the customer who returns a defective product at a local store. When you receive a complaint, remember that it is valuable information. Stop what you are doing. For example, your business is in Michigan. You receive a letter from a woman in Idaho who sent you a check two weeks ago and never received her products. Review the complaint—find out when you shipped the product and how it was shipped. After looking into the complaint, you find that the product was shipped seven days ago, and it was shipped by first-class

```
                        Alan's Mail Order
                          0 Maine Ave.
                          Rusty, MI 0001
                          508-686-0000


    Ms. Sandi O'Neill
    Box 0000
    Oldtown, CA


    Dear Ms. O'Neill:

    Sorry about the shipping delay on your book 199 Time-Waster

    Situations.  We received your order July 6th, and shipped it

    first class on July 7th.  You should receive it shortly.  I'm

    sorry about any inconvenience.  Thank you for your order.


                                    Sincerely,

                                    Alan Wall
```

Fig. 13-3. Use this sample complaint letter to inform your customer about the complaint. A timely reply to customer complaints is essential to success in this business. The customer expects good service.

mail. Write a letter responding to the complaint, and send it without delay. A sample complaint letter is given in Fig. 13-3.

Send the answer to the complaint on the same day you receive it. You cannot do any more important work in your mail-order business than handling complaints from irate customers. Each day you permit the complaint to go unanswered increases the chance for the customer to contact the postal service, the Better Business Bureau, or even the Federal Trade Commission. The Federal Trade Commission requires that any customer paying by check is entitled to have their purchase shipped within 30 days, or they must be notified and given the option to cancel. A customer located thousands of miles away might get nervous if they send you a check for a product, you cash the check, and the customer fails to receive shipment for a few weeks. It is much easier to deal with your customer immediately than waiting too long, only to deal with multiple complaints from the postal service, the Better Business Bureau, or other authorities.

If you run out of your product or service, and you will not get another shipment in for a week or two, inform your customer about the delay before you cash the check. By telling the customer of the situation, the customer can decide whether or not he or she wants to wait the extra time or wants the money refunded. The key to solving complaints is to act promptly and treat the customer fairly at all times.

HOW TO DEAL WITH A CUSTOMER WHO
DEMANDS SHIPMENT, BUT NEVER ORDERED FROM YOU

Almost every mail-order business running advertisements in mail-order magazines will receive letters about fulfilling orders that were never received. Check
out the request completely. If, after checking your files, you find you have no
record that an order was received, ask for proof, such as a cancelled check or
money order. You can use a letter such as the one in Fig. 13-4.

```
                    Diane's Catalog House
                       P.O. Box 0000
                  Huntington Beach, CA   90009


Order:_____


Dear Customer:
I was sorry to hear that you hadn't received your order.
However, when your request for a replacement order was
being processed, we were unable to find a record of your
order in our files.  Therefore, I regret that I must ask
you to send a photostatic copy of both sides of the can-
celled check or money order as proof of purchase.

I am sorry for any inconvenience and assure you that upon
receipt of proof of purchase, your order will be mail im-
mediately.

                              Sincerely,

                              Diane Smithhurst
                              Customer Relations
```

Fig. 13-4. Expect some requests for products or services without receiving a payment. Use
a letter similar to the one above to put the burden of proof of payment on the customer.

KEEP A COMPLAINT FILE

Everyone in mail order will receive a complaint occasionally. When you handle it
quickly, the complaint will go away. The complaints that continue over and over
again will hurt you and your business. Just sending letters will not be enough to
solve the problem. Find out why these complaints persist, and make the necessary changes. For example, Sue B. of Mississippi sold jewelry by mail, and in her
letter, she told her customers she would ship their order within 48 hours after
receiving the order. Instead, Sue was shipping the orders in seven days after
receiving the order. The customers wrote many angry letters, until Sue started
shipping within 48 hours to conform to the promise in the letter. Fulfill your
promise. If you cannot fulfill the promise, do not state it in the first place. Your
customer will demand you fulfill the terms you made in your offer. To keep track

of customer complaints, keep a complaint file, with spaces to write in the date, the nature of the complaint, the solution, and any other remarks.

Modern customer service means more than writing letters, answering the phone, and wrestling complaints. It means giving satisfaction. The customer will continue to buy from you if you offer satisfaction and turn an unhappy customer into a happy one. The unhappy customer will tell others about the unpleasant experience with your company, and may write to a newspaper or an association to multiply the complaint. Keep your cool, tell the customer you want to solve the problem, see things the customer's way, and keep the customer satisfied and buying from you.

CONTINUE TO ADVERTISE

The mail-order businesses that succeed continue to advertise month after month, year after year. Some mail-order owners start with very small advertisements, then they move to larger and larger advertisements—some even purchase full-page ads. Continue to put your money back into advertisements to increase your profits. Advertising cost should be between 15 percent to 20 percent of your total sales. Let's say you want to do $10,000 for your first year. You should try to spend $1,500 to $2,000 for your advertising. Too often, mail-order owners start their business by advertising strongly, but just when the orders increase, they reduce their advertising and their sales decrease as well. Advertising is the motor that drives your mail-order business.

Advertising takes time to work. Many beginning mail-order owners run a few advertisements and expect substantial results. When you run your first ad, give the prospect time to think about your product or service. It may require running this advertisement another time before the reader will respond with an order or a request for more information.

Your advertising program must create in your propect's mind a sense of urgency. Use words to create a need to act *today*. There are specific words that your advertisement must use to develop this sense of urgency such as:

- Act now
- Deadline
- Don't delay
- Golden opportunity
- Last chance
- Limited offer
- Offer expires
- Prices going up
- Time running out

These words show there is a sense of time and limited availability to your offer. Review your advertisement to see whether or not there is sufficient urgency in your advertising program. Check your sales letter, reply card, brochure, and your classified advertisement, as well.

SUCCESSFUL MAIL-ORDER PEOPLE KEEP LEARNING

Each day requires you to examine your mail-order business and make a decision on what you need to do to keep on the right track. For example, have you received any inquiries today? How many orders did you receive? When will you place additional advertisements for your business? When will you make another mailing to your current buyers? What are the new products and services advertising in mail-order magazines? Learn something new about your business daily and use it. People are successful in this business because they have an extraordinary determination to succeed.

ADD SWEEPSTAKES CONTESTS TO YOUR ADVERTISING

These devices may increase your response to the offer. Many people want to win a free gift. The federal anti-lottery laws prohibit sweepstakes that require a purchase. The sweepstakes must accept a plain "3×5" card, or entry equal to the entry that's enclosed with the order card, boxtop, or wrapper. You must consider the cost for administering the sweepstakes or contest in your advertising. Some mail-order owners test the sweepstakes or contest offer and compare the sales results before accepting it fully.

SUMMARY OF KEY POINTS

- Keep your customers buying, your success depends upon it.
- Offer information to your customers to increase your sales revenue.
- Consider special discounts for regular customers.
- Send out a questionnaire to your customers to learn more about them.
- Inform others about your business by speaking to groups and running seminars.
- Good customers require regular offers to keep buying.
- Mail your offer to specific geographic areas.
- Use the power of samples in your business; allowing the customer to see and use a product will improve your chances for success.
- Keep an eye on the calendar; people buy according to the time of year.
- Christmas is an excellent time of year for certain gift products.
- Keep your promises and your focus consistent.
- Combine your inquiries and your direct-mail list together for one mailing.
- Send the inquirer what he expects to receive.
- Consider writing a small article for publication.
- Ask your customers why they did not order.

- Visualize in your mind the average day for your customer.
- You can sell more if you sell to dealers.
- Make your telephone work for you.
- Keep your account current with the supplier of your product.
- Handle irate customers promptly. Set up a system to handle customer complaints.
- Expect letters from people who want shipment, but never ordered from you. Demand proof of their order.
- Keep a complaint file. Look for complaint trends, and take action to solve them.
- Your advertising program must be steady all year long.
- Keep learning new trends and ideas in your business.
- Keep trying new methods to increase your sales.
- Avoid the temptation to copy others.

14

Techniques to Expand Your Business

SOME MAIL-ORDER PEOPLE THINK THE BEST APPROACH TO EXPAND THEIR business is to reach new people. Another important approach is to sell more products and services to your existing customers, while expanding your line of products. For example, Fred O'Neill, a mail-order owner from Tennessee, developed a line of products for career women, including career publications and other products to expand their career success. Fred is currently advertising in over seven magazines monthly, and the business is expanding smoothly. Successful mail-order selling is finding the correct product, directing it towards a target market, and advertising with a clear strategy to sell your customers.

THE PROCESS

Selling in mail order is a process. The process starts with an understanding of the potential customer and ends with receiving a check for an order and shipping the goods. Successful selling is directing all the small and the large things that are necessary to sell your product and keep your customers coming back again and again. It is showing how your product or service can fulfill basic needs, such as food, health, security, and rest. It is showing how your product or service can assure your customer that he or she will feel like an important part of the family, the church, and the community. Good selling also includes the unknown needs the product or service satisfies in the marketplace. It is striking just the right cord to motivate the customer to buy your product or service.

SELLING WITH A FAX MACHINE

Some of your customers want their product immediately. In order to service this segment, permit them to use the fax machine to order for speedy delivery. Facsimiles machines, also called fax machines, can electronically send a letter or purchase order to you in seconds. Your customer can respond to you in seconds, without waiting for the post office to deliver the mail. Even if you don't have a fax machine of your own, you can use a fax machine of a local mailing company in your area. These mailing centers will accept and send your messages for a fee. The use of the fax machines will increase during the next two decades. Consider using the fax machine in your sales letter or catalog to permit your customers these important benefits.

BOUNCE-BACK OFFERS

When you send a package to a customer who just bought your product, send some information on your latest product or your catalog of products to keep the customer buying from you. This practice is similar to the large retailers and banks that send advertising stuffers and brochures when they send your statement for the month. This is an excellent device to increase sales in your business, because you are directing the message to customers who know you, and your product or service. This is also a good opportunity to inform your customer about your new products and when your fall or spring catalog will be available. Your bounce-back offer is an excellent method to keep your customers thinking about your product or service.

SPECIALTY ADVERTISING CAN INCREASE SALES

Have you ever picked up a book of matches at your local restaurant? Do you have a calendar or appointment book with a company name on it? Does your key ring have an advertising message on it? If your answer is ''yes'' to any of these questions, you have received specialty advertising. Specialty advertising is when useful articles, such as matches, pens, combs, calendars, nail clippers, tee shirts, and others carry the advertiser's name, address, and advertising message. The concept behind this advertising is that each time the article is used, the customer is exposed to it. The customer can see, feel, and use the article on a daily, weekly, monthly, even yearly basis.

You determine who receives the specialty advertising items. For example, when your customer purchases at least $75 of products or services from you, you can send him a calendar with your name, address, telephone number, and advertising message on it. Once a year, or on a regular basis, you can send advertising specialties to your target market. For example, an insurance company sends attractive calendars to new businesses in their area. An auto dealer offers attractive and useful key rings to customers and others who are interested in their automobiles.

Some mail-order owners sell specialty advertising to businesses both large and small. Every business can benefit with some specialty advertising to remind others about their products or services. Use specialty advertising to tell your story, and keep your message in front of your customer at all times. Make certain that your advertising specialties are directed at people who are interested in your product; don't just give them out to anyone.

INCREASING SALES MEANS PICKING UP NEW CUSTOMERS REGULARLY

The mail-order businesses that expand and grow profitable year after year do so because they do what is necessary to attract and keep new customers. Like it or not, customers move away, change their mind, become ill, get divorced, get married, and for a number of other reasons, stop purchasing from you. To stay successful, you are required to get new customers to make up for the ones you lose. In an earlier chapter we talked about knowledge of your target market. What magazines does he or she read today? Are you advertising in these magazines? Are you aware of the new and emerging markets to increase your business. For example, one mail-order owner who sells products on part-time jobs and careers is now selling to retired people living in Florida and California. These retired people have both the money and the time to buy these mail-order products and services. It is not enough to know your product or service and target market, you must keep up with changing market conditions.

USE A PREMIUM TO INCREASE BUSINESS

A premium is a special offer to help sell your product or service. It is used in a sales promotion to give the customer a reason to buy your product or service. A premium can be directed towards your present customers, dealers, or a special target market such as writers. The premium might be a free pen when the customer buys your stationery. It might be a drinking glass for the purchase of cookware, or free toothpaste with the purchase of a toothbrush. Some mail-order people find premiums work better than giving discounts on their prices. Many customers feel that when they have a choice of a premium, they will "get something for nothing."

Premiums are very important to your sales effort. Give premiums the necessary time and effort to make them pay off for your company. The premium has an advantage of increasing the value of the product, and, at the same time, decreasing the cost of the product, because two products are given for the price of one. For example, if you sell a subscription to your $24-a-year newsletter, and the premium is a special book on careers, with a value of $4, you are increasing the value and lowering the price. This is a very powerful sales incentive for you. Choose the premium carefully; if it fails to work, change it until it works. Once you find a premium that works, use it until sales drop off.

USE THE "WHAT IF" GAME

Many mail-order people play a game called "What If" to determine their goals for the future. What if you sold 1,000 units a month rather than 700? What if you used a more attractive premium and sold 1,100 units? You can increase profits by increasing the amount of units sold, and by decreasing the price you pay for each unit. For example, if you spent $2 for a set of earrings, and you sell them for $6, you earn a profit of $4. On the other hand, when you purchase the same-quality earrings for $1, and you sell them for $6, you earn a profit of $5. By playing the "What If" game, you can set higher goals for yourself, and increase your profit and sales.

LISTEN CAREFULLY TO YOUR CUSTOMERS

Good selling requires excellent listening skills and remembering that the customer talks to you both verbally and nonverbally. For example, when you send a sales letter and brochure to your inquirer, and you fail to get a reply or a check, the package failed to do the job. Why did the inquirer fail to respond to your offer? The inquirer is communicating to you by not responding to your offer. Perhaps offering the product again will increase your returns. Mail-order people must consider the reason for the nonverbal objection. Your job is to close all the doors to the objections. Once your offer handles the objections, you will receive the order.

Pay attention to any letters you receive from your customers or your inquirers. What are they telling you in those letters? Is there any confusion? For example, I received some letters from people who were confused about the product being sold. I revised the sales letter to make the offer clearer. Your mail-order business needs this valuable input from your customers. Try to keep a record of these comments about your business, and when you see a trend on certain comments, you can make the necessary adjustments to increase the sales. For example, are the customers confused about your price? Do they ask about your policy on shipping charges? Do they ask about the guarantee of your product or service? Many sales are lost because the potential customer is confused by your offer. When the customer likes the products, can see important benefits in it, and understands the terms, the sale will be easier to complete. Listen carefully to everything the customer asks you about the product, make necessary corrections and your sales will increase.

INCREASE SALES BY GETTING THE CUSTOMER TO BUY TODAY

Today is everything. When the customer hesitates to respond to your offer the day it arrives, your chances of selling your product or service are lessened. Make *today* count in your mail-order business by asking the prospect to make a decision to buy "today." Be friendly, but with a business-oriented approach, and ask the prospect for the order. The prospect may not buy unless you ask for the order. Make certain you communicate benefits and advantages for buying today. Suggest to your customer the benefits of showing your quality product or service to their friends and family. Be willing to sell the sizzle instead of the steak. Make your offer so attractive your customer cannot refuse it.

Use a "Let's Get Acquainted" special deal to motivate the customer or prospect to buy today. For example, a mail-order owner in the services business gives some free gifts and a discount on a 60-minute audio tape to make his offer more attractive. These gifts, plus the discount on the tape, is increasing his number of customers and sales in the business. Show a genuine interest in your prospect and ask for the opportunity to sell to him or her today.

KNOW YOUR PRODUCTS OR SERVICES

Many mail-order owners start their business with a great deal of enthusiasm and learn all about their products and services. Soon after, they begin spending their time in other areas, and their product knowledge grows stale and out-of-date. To sell to today's customers requires a firm knowledge of the products and services of your business. For example, I have a friend who changed careers and started selling automobiles. His first few weeks on the job were difficult because he didn't know the products; he was unfamiliar with the numerous models and accessories. He spent some time reading about the models and watched them on the road while driving back and forth to work. Once he knew the products, he felt more comfortable and continued to probe deeper and deeper into the benefits of each model. My friend was hungry for information and absorbed it like a giant sponge. With this enthusiasm and knowledge, he is now one of the best sales representatives in the auto agency. In your mail-order business, make an effort to keep fresh on your product knowledge—how your products stand out from others and how they can benefit the customer. When adding new products and services to your line, be sure to tell your customers why you're selling these products and explain to them the benefits of the products completely. Don't assume the customers are familiar with your products, continue to tell your story over and over until you succeed. In mail order, knowledge is power.

SPEND MORE TIME IN YOUR BUSINESS

I received a call recently from a friend who started her own mail-order business last year. She was unhappy about the lack of growth of her business. I asked her how much time she spends in the business and her answer was only a few hours per week. In order to make your business grow requires an investment in time and effort. Only *you* can make your mail-order business work. The best way to make it work is to spend as much time as possible in your business.

Send out those inquiries on a daily basis, and send a regular mailing to keep the sales coming in. Pay regular attention to your business so that you get a complete understanding of your customer's needs. Spend an hour each day, and spend some time on the weekend on your business. Once you spend time each day, it will become a habit, which will, in turn, become a workstyle and an important part of your life.

EXAMINE YOUR OFFERS

What is the reaction to your offers? One mail-order owner gets reactions to his offer from six people, which he calls his "insider group." It includes friends, relatives, and associates. Once he makes a mailing, he makes certain that each member of his insider group gets a copy of it. He then calls each member of the group and will ask the following questions:

- When did you receive the offer?
- Did it look professional?
- Was it easy to read?
- Were the terms easy to understand?
- Did the mailing make it easy to act?
- Was the price attractive, and within your means?
- Any other comments?

The insider's group gives you the needed information to determine whether or not the message was easy to understand and if it made a favorable impression on the readers. Be willing to accept criticism from the group. This insider's group can give you added information to keep your mailing package working for you rather than against you.

Now let's sum up.

SUMMARY OF KEY POINTS

- Selling is a process. Be sure to know and understand this process—from the mental stage to the physical stage.

- Successful selling does not just happen, it requires hard work and a complete understanding of the consumer.
- The fax machine is now important in the selling process.
- Bounce-back selling means sending new offers to your customers in the same packages you ship their product to them.
- Put your knowledge into action.
- Offer premiums to increase your sales. You need people to try your product so that you can develop a favorable reputation. Sometimes the premiums help you to do so.
- Listen carefully to all remarks about your product or service.
- Ask your customer to buy today, not tomorrow.
- Use "Get Acquainted" offers.
- Know your product or service better than your competition.
- Spend the necessary time in your business.

15

Managing Your Business
Successfully

A MAIL-ORDER BUSINESS AT HOME MUST BE MANAGED JUST AS A LARGE business with hundreds of employees. Keep your successful advertisements running and the cash-flow moving correctly while shipping the products, other offers, and catalogs promptly. You must know the cost of your product or service, and the difference between the product and the marketing costs. Try to look beyond the daily happenings in your mail-order business and make the necessary decisions to allow your business to grow in the future.

KEEP TRACK OF YOUR SALES

Control your revenues in your business. Revenues are the amount of sales you earn in your business—in other words, the amount of products or services. For example, if you sell 100 designer watches at $49 each for the month of March, your sales will be $4,900 dollars. Your sales records can tell you a great deal more about your business than a dollar amount; they can give you information on what products or services are selling. For example, are you selling more watches or rings in your business? Why are you selling more watches? Are you running more advertisements for your watches than for your rings? Are you trying to sell more watches by running more advertisements and sending more information on them? The table on p. 164 shows how you can break down your

Breaking Down Sales by Product or Service

	January	February	March	Total	% of Total
Watches	75	50	100	225	69%
Rings	25	35	40	100	31%
TOTAL	100	85	140	325	100%

sales by product or service. It shows that over two-thirds of your sales for the quarter (the first 3 months of the year) are from your watches, and only 31 percent of your sales are from your rings.

Your sales records can also give you important management information, such as what advertisements and magazines are bringing in the business. Why keep running advertisements in magazines that are not generating the sales for you? Review your sales records regularly, so you can determine what advertisements and magazines are working for you. The table below breaks down the sales by the magazine and advertisement.

Breaking Down Sales by Magazine or Advertisement

	Watches	Rings	Advertisement #
Publication A	75	—	1 D (Display)
Publication B	—	70	2 C (Classified)
Publication C	100	—	3 D
Publication D	—	5	4 C
Publication E	—	15	6 C
Publication F	—	10	5 D
Publication G	50	—	7 C
TOTAL	225	100	

MAIL ORDER REQUIRES CONTINUOUS TESTING

An important part of mail order is the continuous testing of the important elements in your business. For example, which product or products are selling for you? Which lists are working for you? What is the best offer? Which mailing package is pulling the most sales for you? Successful management of your business requires testing of a variety of elements of your mail-order business. Test one element at a time. For example, if you want to test your sales letter, send out 1,000 mailing packages with sales letter A, and 1,000 mailing packages using sales letter B. (Your order card can be keyed with an A or B to designate the sales letter used.) Check the results.

ASK SOMEONE TO READ YOUR ADVERTISEMENT ALOUD

A mail-order owner in Indiana lets her daughter read the sales letter aloud to get the full benefit of the message. By hearing her advertisement and sales letter, it was easier to pick out the sales letter she wanted to use for a trial mailing. One sales letter focused on the safety features of the product, and when used in a trial mailing, pulled 5 percent. This sales letter is still being used. Once you find a good-pulling sales letter or mailing package that works, continue to work with it.

AVERAGE SALES SIZE

The average sale is very important to your business success. It is very expensive to gain a customer in mail order. This is why it is so important to sell as much as possible to build your business. Determining your average sale will help you gauge your success. For example, when you sell 200 customers in one month and you receive $2,100 in sales, the average sales size is $10.50. Perhaps the customer is only purchasing your manual you sell for $10 and buying other products from other mail-order catalogs. Your challenge will be to increase your average sales size to a higher level.

One approach you can use is to upgrade your products or service, so you can increase your price and still show value to your customer. For example, for a number of years I sold a manual on newsletters for $10, and my average sales size was about $12. I knew I needed to increase it. I changed the manual into a course by adding additional information to the original product. By adding this additional feature to the product, I increased the price to $30. Review your average sales size on a monthly basis to determine how your products and services are selling. The table below shows you how to determine your average sales size.

Average Sales Size for January, February, March

	Units	Price	Totals
Product A	50	$ 5.00	$225.00
Product B	25	12.00	300.00
Product C	32	20.00	640.00
Product D	40	6.00	240.00
TOTAL	147		$1,405.00

Average Sales Size 147 ÷ $1,405.00 = $9.56

FIND YOUR SPECIAL CUSTOMERS AND REWARD THEM

Mail-order success means maintaining a good relationship with your customers. "Heavy users" are the customers who buy more than other customers. Treat those special customers in a manner that will make them feel special. For example, a catalog operation compiled a list of customers who bought more than $1,000 worth of merchandise in the previous year. The owner of the business sent these people a wallet and a credit card calculator, along with a letter stating "We appreciate your business and want you to know we care about you." Purchases during the next year by these special customers increased over 35 percent.

Never take your excellent customers for granted. Good customers with good purchasing power are very important to you, and many other mail-order people are trying to take them away from you. Keep sending them better offers, and keep them buying from you. Find reasons why these important customers should keep buying from you rather than your competition. Repeat business is essential to your mail-order success. Your customers will keep buying if you sell high-quality products, ship promptly, handle customer complaints professionally, and refund money quickly.

MAKE SURE YOUR TEST GROUP IS LARGE ENOUGH

Too often the mail-order owner mails out 100 direct-mail packages to random names on list A, to determine whether or not this list will sell the product or service. Since list A contains 50,000 names, the 100 names would not be large enough to determine the future results. Perhaps the 100 names were located in your state. Testing 2,000 to 3,000 names on the list would be much more representative. Small test quantities cannot give you the information you need to make definitive decisions.

AVOID READING NON-TEST FACTORS INTO YOUR RESULTS

You changed the headlines in your sales letter, and increased the amount of testimonials as well. You find that in the month following these changes, you noticed a sharp increase in your returns. Using the two-step method, your direct-mail packages to inquiries increased in returns from 8 percent to 12 percent. What is the reason for the increase? Without testing, you cannot assume you know the answer. Some mail-order people simply try to guess the reason for the increase, instead of doing the required testing. In the table on p. 167, you will find a test showing the two changes in copy, and which one made the most important contribution to the increase in sales results.

Note that the sales letter with new headline increased to 8 percent from 6 percent for the control letter, and the sales letter with testimonials scored 10 percent, beating both sales letters.

Testing Copy Changes

	Number of Inquiries Sent	Number Returned with Order	Percent
Control letter (using old copy)	1,000	60	6%
Sales letter with new headline only	1,000	80	8%
Sales letter with new testimonials only	1,000	100	10%

TEST FOR THE BEST POSSIBLE ADVERTISEMENT

You want to generate the best possible amount of inquiries for your product or services. Do you use classified advertisement A or classified advertisement B? Why not place both advertisements into the same issue of a mail-order magazine and find out which advertisement generates the most inquiries that turn into sales. Inquiries are not enough; you must have inquiries that generate orders.

Testing Advertisements

	Amount of Inquiries	% Converted into Sales	Total Sales
Advertisement A	150	10%	15
Advertisement B	140	8%	11

Advertisement A shows a 10 percent conversion of inquiries into sales, it beat the advertisement B by a full 2 percent. If you place the advertisement A in more magazines, your total sales will be higher for you.

AVOID TOO MUCH TESTING

Test only the essential elements in your mail-order business. For example, it is important to determine which advertisement is working for you. It is not essential to determine what is the best color for your envelope. Focus on the important parts of your business. What is the best copy for your letter? What is the best offer? What about the price? What is the best list to sell your product or service? What is the best direct-mail format to sell your product better? Test the essentials rather than the trivial to make your business work.

THE COST PER THOUSAND READERS

Do you use magazine A or magazine B to run your advertisement? One way to determine which magazine you should use is to determine the cost to reach a thousand readers. Mail-order owners use the cost-per-thousand formula to watch costs. The table below will show you how to determine the cost per thousand, also called CPT.

The mail-order business is a numbers business. The more people who see your product or service advertised, the better the opportunity to sell it.

Determining Cost per Thousand

	Circulation	Advertisement Cost	CPT
Magazine Z	200,000	$ 50.00	.25
Magazine F	100,000	125.00	1.25
Magazine V	500,000	175.00	.35

The Magazine Z will cost $.25 per thousand
readers versus $1.25 for Magazine F.

MAIL OUT ALL PIECES AT THE SAME TIME

It would be unfair to test the accuracy of one list against the other, unless you send all pieces at the same time. Let's say, for example, the test was done in December. Some pieces were sent out in the first week of the month, and the remainder sent out a few days before Christmas. Mail received just before or after Christmas can change your results. People will not order products a few days before an important holiday. Weather can also have an effect on your results. Try to get all your mailing pieces to your post office at the same time.

DO THE TEST OVER AGAIN

To avoid making important changes based on just one test, you might consider doing the test over again to avoid the possibility that some unusual circumstance has prejudiced the test results. Some mail-order people call this "two-flight testing." This is extra work, and an extra expense, but respected mail-order field professionals contend this practice is a necessary safeguard.

TEST THE OFFER

Your offer is the most important element in your mail-order business. One mail-order company tested two offers in the example below. One offered a free booklet, and the other was a standard inquiry-producing offer.

	% of Inquiries	Sales
Offer A (with Free Booklet)	4.6%	9,310.00
Offer B (Standard Offer no special inducement)	3.3%	10,000.00

The results showed the free booklet offer generated a higher percentage of inquiries than the standard offer. But, when the mail-order company tested the convertibility to sales, the standard offer had $10,000 sales to only $9,310 for the free booklet special offer. Inquiries are important, but the sales are more important.

TEST ITEMS REFUSED OR RETURNED FOR CREDIT

Why are certain products being returned? Are these returned goods purchased reluctantly just to get the free booklet or other free gift incentive you offered? Examine the goods returned on a regular basis to determine the possible reasons. Perhaps the customer felt the value of the product did not represent the cost of the product.

Expect a 5 percent return of mail-order products. When the percentage is higher, examine the product carefully, along with the price, advertisements, copy, offer, and your mail list. The 5 percent return rate means that for every 100 products you sell, five are being returned to you. Any return rate above 5 percent will require some research to find the reason for it.

Returns are expensive. Not only are you required to take the product back and put it into inventory, but usually the product is used because of the double shipment and extra handling. You are also required to send the customer a check for the returned product. The check must be made promptly so the customer knows you want to deal with him or her in a professional manner.

WHAT IS A CREDIT?

A credit means that you are accepting the customer's return of goods and you will adjust your records accordingly. Let's say, for example, your customer, Ms. Brown from Brooklyn, New York returned a watch for $35. You will send her the check for $35, if she requests it, or you could apply the $35 credit on a future purchase. When Ms. Brown reorders from your catalog again and spends $100, you can deduct the $35 and the cost to the customer will only be $65. Ask your customer whether they want the check or the credit to avoid any misunderstanding. A steady customer may be willing to accept the credit from you.

A MAIL-ORDER YARDSTICK: PERCENT OF RETURN

Percent of return is one of the most important and most commonly used yardsticks in the business today. This figure is determined by taking the number of pieces mailed and the number of orders received. The formula is the following:

$$\text{Percent of Return} = \frac{\text{Number of Orders Received}}{\text{Total number of Pieces Mailed}}$$

For example, you are using the direct-mail method of selling, and you send 1,000 direct-mail pieces to your house list and receive 20 orders. To determine your percent of return you can do the following mail-order math:

$$\frac{20}{1000} = 2\% \text{ of Return}$$

For every hundred pieces you sent to your customers, you received back two orders. Does this mean you made a profit? Remember: a profit is the difference between your revenue and your expenses. In order to determine if the 2 percent return is profitable for you, the cost of your mailing and the fulfillment (product or service costs) must be included. The percent of return, in itself, is not enough to determine profits; you also need other information to give a profit and loss.

THE COST PER ORDER

The cost per order is another very important yardstick in the mail-order business. This is the cost of attaining an order. Some mail-order owners feel that the cost per order is the most important consideration available. The cost per order is determined with the following formula:

$$\text{Cost per Order} = \frac{\text{Total Cost of Mailing}}{\text{Number of Orders Received}}$$

For example, you decide to mail 2,000 mailing pieces at a cost of $460. You receive 30 orders for that mailing. To determine your cost per order you can do the following mail-order math:

$$\frac{\$460}{30} = \$15.33 \text{ Cost per Order}$$

Selling your product to your customer will cost you $15.33 and, remember, this figure does not include the cost of your product or service itself. If you are using the two-step method of selling, you will determine your cost per order by adding your advertising costs for the magazines, and adding the cost to send out the piece mailed to your potential customers. For example, let's say your small advertisement in a magazine cost $75, and you received 100 inquiries, with a cost of postage and printing costs of $45. You receive 25 orders. To determine your cost per order:

$$\frac{\$120}{25} = \text{Cost per Order } \$4.80$$

To carry the value of cost per order further, add your cost of the product to this figure, and you will find the total unit cost for your product. Let's say your product cost is $5.87, so you add this amount to the cost per order of $4.80, for a total of $10.67. If a $15.99 selling price is used, you need 17 orders to break even. Let's look at the math:

	Costs	Math Breakdown
Advertising & Postage	$120.00	$75 advertising $45 postage & printing pieces
Cost of Product	$146.75	25 × $5.87
TOTAL	$266.75	

$$\frac{\text{Total Costs}}{\text{Selling Price}} = \frac{\$266.75}{\$15.99} = 17 \text{ Orders (Amount needed to break even)}$$

You need at least 17 orders to break even—after that, you will begin to earn profits. As a mail-order manager, you should understand what you need to break even, so you can establish a quota for each advertisement or mailing. You want to not only break even, but sell as many units as possible above it. Be aggressive. Don't only try to break even, strive to exceed it.

COMBINE THE ELEMENTS TOGETHER FOR SUCCESS

You are in charge of getting things together. In your own mail-order business, this means putting the best products, offers, packages, magazines, and lists together to work for you. Combine the best selection into a winning campaign to keep your sales growing. For example, review your offer. Is your offer attractive? How does the offer compare with your competition? Are you keeping up with the changes in your field? Too often mail-order people find a formula that works, and they continue to use it even when it becomes obsolete. It's no secret that your customers know what they want, and they expect your best efforts. Your customers will not accept your second best. They will go to a competitor if your offer fails to reach them. Your job will be to please them fully.

I attended a seminar recently, and the seminar leader made a very clear point: The cow never stays milked, you must milk the cow over and over. In the mail-order business, you are like the farmer, you must continue to keep your mail-order business changing to meet the demands of the customer. Only *you* can keep your business fresh and alive by reaching for new things to help service your customer.

Never take your customer for granted. Your customer is always changing—you must also change to meet these new demands. Be willing to change hats. Put on the hat of your customer. Put your mailing piece into your mailbox, pick it up with your regular mail, and read it over as a potential customer. Does your mailing piece get you excited enough to fill out the order card and send a check as well? It is very easy to fall into complacency, lose momentum, and let your profits slide. For example, one mail-order owner in Florida, recently changed the look of her catalog to reflect a more professional look, and offered fewer products to give the customer a chance to order more quality-oriented products. The Florida mail-order dealer was willing to make changes to keep the owner and customer relationship a stronger one. Show the customer you care.

GOOD MAIL-ORDER MANAGERS
SPECIALIZE ON ONE STRONG AREA

I like the story of the old lady, Mae Jones, from Maine that knitted special heavy-duty sweaters for skiers. She used unique colors and exciting knitting patterns that gained her a following all over the state of Maine. She started to sell by mail order, and her business grew in leaps and bounds. A friend suggested she try other knitting products to go along with the ski sweaters, such as pillow cases, socks, and scarves. All these new products were tried, but the experiment resulted in a lack of attention to the ski sweaters that started the success in the first place. Mae decided to stick to her most important product. The business was soon back on track, because the focus returned to the most important area. This story is important because it uncovers an important rule in mail order: specialize in one area, and keep working to become known as the best mail-order dealer for this specialized area. Avoid the temptation of expanding your product offering so wide that you compromise your quality and service. Your customer does not care about your business problems, they just want the best product at the best price. Your goal is to give your customer their money's worth, so they come back for more.

IDEAS ARE YOUR STOCK-IN-TRADE

The most valuable attributes you can develop as a mail-order owner is a creative mind, a creative spirit, and a confidence to try new things. Be willing to try some new things—even with the possibility they may fail. New ideas might mean trying a new mailing list of buyers. It might mean trying different mail-order magazines. It might mean simply presenting your product in a different way than in the past. It might mean joining one product with another to increase sales. It might mean developing a theme for your product to give your customers a new chance to see your products or services in a different light. For example, one mail-order owner changed the theme to "The Next-Generation Company." Another mail-order owner stresses "New Age Products." Still another mail-order owner from Maine developed a theme called "Quality Products from the State of Maine" to keep his customers interested.

How do you come up with new ideas? This is one of the most popular questions in my mail-order seminars. One way is to spend some time to think about how you can make your business better. Review other mail-order offers. Just what is the competition doing today? Instead of copying their idea, simply use it as a springboard to make your business better. Come up with ideas to help your product or service stand out from the competition. It might mean offering a special offer with your product, or it might mean free booklets or even free shipping for a set amount of time.

Your idea will have a greater chance to succeed if you use your past knowledge and experience to build upon your idea. For example, Irene M. of Wisconsin recently retired from a large manufacturing company, after working as a secretary for over 35 years. She wanted to develop some products or services for the people in a field she knows a great deal about: secretaries. Irene's idea was to develop a line of products especially designed for them, such as calculators, books, and office and stationery items. This former secretary's idea blends delightfully with her background, interests, and experience. Irene is planning to start a small catalog within the next few years to put all the products together. This example, shows you how to tie your idea with your past experiences and knowledge.

MEND YOUR MAIL-ORDER FENCES REGULARLY

In the mail-order business, like any other business, you must be willing to keep the people happy all around you. For example, let's say you have a fight with your printer or with your supplier; take the time and effort to mend those fences. By contacting the printer and showing a genuine concern for putting the fight behind you, you will give yourself the flexibility of using the printer in the future. Don't put so much pressure on your suppliers that you have no other suppliers in the area who will do business with you.

One mail-order owner mends his fences during the summer, and gets all his suppliers in line for the fall season. When a family member helps you in your mail-order business, and you have a disagreement, take the time to mend the situation before it gets out of hand. You cannot do everything yourself. You need the help of others. Mend fences to keep your business together.

THE LOST LEADER METHOD

The lost leader method is a device to increase your business by offering your customer more for his or her money. Many mail-order operations, book clubs, associations, and other businesses use this method with success. The lost leader is when you sell a product at a lower price to increase future sales. The idea behind the lost leader method is to get the customer to try your product with the possibility of future sales of your other products or services. Each sale of the lost leader gives you an excellent opportunity to follow up with brochures, sales letters, and other offers, and your profit comes along with these important additional sales.

Choose a product that best represents your line of products, is worthwhile, and is an excellent value. Make the offer attractive, so the customer will buy it. Once the lost leader is sold, you will have a chance to offer your full presentation with your other products or services. One mail-order owner from Oklahoma finds that by using the lost leader method, he can offer the buyer a sample to demonstrate the high quality of the products.

The lost leader method helps you to identify the best prospects for your business. For example, if your lost leader is a book on home decorating, selling for $3, the customers will be people interested in decorating their own homes, or going into the business of home decorating. Now, you can sell your home decorating products. This lost leader method simply matches the product with the best possible buyer. (This idea was discussed earlier in the book.) Be sure to remember this principle: Each day your main job as a manager of your business is continuing to select the best possible customers, who have the desire and the money to buy, and then match them to your quality products or services.

CONTROL YOUR INVENTORY

As a manager of your inventory, you want to purchase enough inventory so you do not run out of products. On the other hand, you want to avoid excessive inventory. The best inventory method is to have products on-hand, without excessive storage. An excellent method is to base your inventory on your expected sales for the month. For example, let's say you expect to sell 100 products per week, or 400 products per month. Make certain that you keep at least 400 to 500 products on-hand to cover your shipping requirements. Keep in mind that you cannot expect your supplier to ship your products out immediately when you run out of products. Set a minimum product level, such as 125. When your supply reaches this number, reorder more products. This 125 figure is only slightly more than one week's sales, so reorder immediately, and remember that if you delay, you may run out of products, and your customers will be angry. It is to your advantage to have an overstock of products, rather than too few.

WHAT TO DO WHEN YOU RUN OUT OF PRODUCTS

Take first things first: order your products immediately. When you receive an order from a customer, hold the check—never deposit it until you know you can ship the product. If you determine that it will take longer than a few days for the customer to receive your product, write a letter or short note about the situation. Tell the customer you ran out of products, and it will delay shipment of his order by a few days. Then ask him or her whether the delay is acceptable, or if he or she would like the check returned. Give the customer a choice. Once you give the customer a choice, you can follow through on their decision, and the chances for a more agreeable conclusion are better.

Never, and this must be repeated, *never* cash a check for an order and delay the delivery of the product or service. This is very upsetting to the customer. He or she receives the cancelled check in a bank statement, and then finds the product was never delivered. Their first impression is that you run an unprofessional mail-order organization, and the second impression is that you are trying to run away with their money. Always write to them right away, and hold the check until you ship. This practice will keep you on the best side of your customer. Strive for service that works for your customer. Become a customer-pleaser.

Sloppy service with your customers, including late and incorrect shipments, will cause you a great deal of trouble. Dealing with unhappy customers is both expensive in time and in money. Unhappy customers will call you on the telephone, write nasty letters, write to their local Better Business Bureau, and alert government officials at the Federal Trade Commission. Sloppy service does something else: it tarnishes your reputation, and your customers will go elsewhere with their orders and their money. One large mail-order company fell behind his shipments to customers because of horrid, snowy, cold winter weather. He tried to contact his customers to tell them about the delay, but with the circumstances of bad weather and computer trouble, he fell behind. Customers wrote letters to the Federal Trade Commission, and after an investigation, the mail-order owner was fined thousands of dollars. Why take the chance of sliding deeper into trouble? Stay ahead of your shipments, make service a priority, keep the customer's interest in mind, and you can avoid excessive problems.

DO A MAIL-ORDER ANALYSIS REGULARLY

Just as you tune your automobile periodically to keep it running smoothly, your mail-order business requires a regular analysis to keep it working up to the maximum. This means reviewing the results of your mail-order advertisement—checking the total response to your advertisements, looking at the total sales from the advertisements, and carefully checking whether your copy is believable and whether you are making a profit or a loss on each advertisement.

Sometimes mail-order owners take their advertisements to an outside advertising agency or a consultant to perform this analysis for them. Try to do the analysis yourself. But be sure to do it on a regular basis, so you can make the necessary corrections in the business.

USE SCORE FOR OUTSIDE HELP

The United States Government spends a great deal of money to help small-business people succeed in their businesses. In order to accomplish this goal, they established SCORE, a service corps of retired executives with a prime goal of assisting small-business people with free counseling. The corp is comprised of people with special expertise in accounting, law, banking, sales, and manufacturing. One office in Massachusetts even includes a patent attorney. Each counselor has a specific area of expertise. They call on companies and hold seminars and workshops. Some counselors even discourage some people from going into business. Some people lack the planning, knowledge, or the desire to learn what they need to learn, or simply lack the persistence needed to survive.

The real benefit of the SCORE agency is the fee cost. There is no fee—it's free. It was developed to help small businesses that cannot afford outside specialists. The office also offers free management aids on various subjects, from accounting to borrowing principles. It also can give you information on loan programs offered by the Small Business Administration. To receive a listing of the free management aids, write to Small Business Administration, P.O. Box 15434, Fort Worth, TX 76119, for information on ordering.

Look up the local SCORE office in your phonebook. Call them to set up a time to discuss your business with them. Ask for a mail-order counselor. It is well worth the price. Take advantage of it.

DON'T FALL FOR GET-RICH SCHEMES

When researching the mail-order business, you will read many advertisements, some of which will offer all sorts of elaborate get-rich ideas. Examples are free radio advertising and free postage. Don't make the time and effort sending for them. Once you get into this habit, it is hard to break. Focus instead on your own mail-order business and work to make it better and better.

YOU ARE THE MANAGER OF YOUR BUSINESS

You are the owner and manager of your business. Managing means keeping the business needs in mind at all times. When you need additional advertising, you take the necessary steps. When you need additional products in your business, you take the action necessary to add to your product line. When your business requires a closer attention to customer service details, it will be up to you to strive for better performance in this area. As the manager, you must be willing to find the leaks in the ship, and then do something to fix the leaks before more extensive repairs are necessary.

As the manager, you can take advantage of the exciting sense of newness when you start your mail-order business. Many consumers enjoy doing business with a new business. Other consumers like the security of doing business with an established business. As a manager, try to bring the old and the new together. Bring the old ideas along with the new ideas. Bring the old products along with some new ones. Bring the old customers along with the new customers. A manager must continually renew himself, or he will fall behind the competition. A good manager not only keeps up with the latest changes in the field, but takes the time and effort to take action. A good manager knows he is a student forever. Learn about new ideas, techniques, methods, products, services, and customer needs even before the customer knows about it. Keep planning ahead.

A good manager keeps a careful watch on how the money is spent in the business. Excessive costs are controlled so that more resources can be spent in areas for growth, such as advertising and new products. Watch those personal costs as well. Keep all the money earned in the business, in the business—especially in the beginning. Try to make the company earn its keep. Keep a separate checking account for your business, and keep it separate from personal finances. By keeping it separate, it will be easier to do your taxes at the end of the year, and easier to determine your expenses and your sales.

Now let's summarize.

SUMMARY OF KEY POINTS

- Know your sales. Know what products and services are selling for you.
- Each product or service must pull a profit.
- Testing is the backbone of the business.
- Read the advertisement aloud.
- Determine your average sales size.
- Find the heavy users, and deliver special offers and rewards to them.
- Be sure to test a large enough segment of your mail list to be representative.
- Test for the best possible advertisements.
- Find the cost per thousand to reach readers.
- Avoid excessive testing.
- Be willing to do a double test.
- Test your offer and items returned to you.
- Know the value of issuing credits.
- The key mail-order yardstick is the percent of return.
- Know your cost per order and your break-even point.
- Keep a specialty.
- Ideas are your stock-in-trade.
- Mend your mail-order fences.
- Use the lost leader method.
- Watch your inventory level.
- Do a mail analysis regularly.

- Use SCORE volunteers, and learn the various services offered by the Small Business Administration.
- Avoid get-rich schemes.
- You are the manager, take the necessary responsibility.

16

Preparing Your Catalog Successfully

YOU CAN SELL A SINGLE PRODUCT OR SERVICE TO BUILD YOUR HOUSE LIST, BUT to give your business the best chances for success, you will need to prepare a catalog showing all your products or services. Your catalog will give you a chance to sell your customers all your products or services and, at the same time, gain their confidence. A customer might spend an hour or more reviewing your products or services. Many mail-order owners find their best customer is the person who recently placed an order with you, and then received your excellent product, which was delivered promptly. This is your opportunity to strike when the iron is hot.

WHAT IS A CATALOG?

The catalog defined is a book, leaflet, or file, containing names, articles and listings. A catalog might be as small as 8 pages or as large as 99 pages. One mail-order owner in Illinois mails spring and fall catalogs of computers and computer supplies—each over 100 pages long. The catalog is your opportunity to show your full line of products in an organized manner.

THE CATALOG HAS LONG LIFE

A catalog, like a magazine, will have long life. It may end up on the coffee table in your customer's house, it might be shown to neighbors, or it might be taken to school to other teachers and students. A catalog offers you an excellent opportunity to expand your market and increase your sales. An attractive catalog becomes an important ambassador of goodwill for you—it will spread the word about your business and products.

CATALOGS EXPAND YOUR BUSINESS

Because catalogs offer a variety of products, they offer your customers or potential customers choices—and people enjoy the buying benefits. Many mail-order businesses grow with a good catalog mailed to a responsive list. An alive list might be a house list, or perhaps a list with people who have a strong need and the purchasing power for your product. For example, a mail-order company in Wisconsin developed an attractive catalog to sell their silk clothing by mail. A mail-order company selling pet supplies in New Jersey expanded their business from $309 a year to $2,500,000 four years later by using a catalog. Another company, selling children's clothing by mail, expanded their sales dramatically by showing their products off in a carefully produced catalog.

PLAN YOUR CATALOG

If your catalog is carefully planned, uses a theme, and stresses product benefits for your customers, it will be received with satisfaction. Use a theme such as ecology, the summer season, the Christmas season, the Easter season, the new season, or one based on national events.

JOIN THE THEME AND THE CUSTOMERS' NEEDS TOGETHER

A successful catalog carefully blends a well-planned theme to the needs of your customers. Answer the following questions fully: Who will use your catalog? What will the catalog do for them? What type of information do your customers need to purchase from you? What products or services will be included in your catalog? What photographs or illustrations will make your catalog work even better? How can you organize items of the same type into the same section of your catalog? What extra information can you include in your catalog to make it easier for the customer to order from you? Remember: the catalog is your sales representative that stays right with your prospect and provides essential information about your business and product. Once you answer the above questions, you can write your own outline to plan your catalog. Refer to the example on p. 181.

Your outline is important because it will make it easier for your customer or prospect to concentrate on specific products or services. Don't make him jump from one group to another. The customer will get confused and turn to something else. A well-developed outline will permit the reader of your catalog to move through each page. Many successful catalogs include copy blocks, broken up into separate units for more interest and readability. Refer to Fig. 16-1 for an example of a layout using the copy block approach.

Copy should include not only the construction features of the product, but should mention the primary functions of the product. Tell your reader where it is used and why the product is better than competitive products.

Attraction Giftware Catalog Outline

A. *Theme*—"Gifts for Your Home and Lifestyle"
B. *Cover*—2/c showing key gifts
C. *Section 1*—Gifts for Home
D. *Section 2*—Gifts for Your Lifestyle
E. *Section 3*—How Gift Can Be Used
F. *Section 4*—Order form; Special 10% Off

PREPARING YOUR CATALOG FOR TYPESETTING

Getting your catalog ready for typesetting will require you to prepare a layout showing the various visual and typeset elements to be included. It will also require a manuscript of all copy included in the catalog. Read the manuscript carefully for spelling and correct grammar before you send it to the typography house. It is much easier to correct a spelling mistake in the proofreading stage, rather than the day after the catalog is printed. Keep a copy of your manuscript, so you can answer any questions that the typography company may have, and in case any copy gets misplaced at the typography house. Be sure to use an experienced, skilled typesetting house. Good typography can save you space in your catalog, and make it easier to read.

WHAT PRODUCTS OR SERVICES SHOULD BE INCLUDED?

Your initial reaction might be to include all your products or services. As your business grows you want to separate certain products into specific sections of your catalog. For example, if your product is used in the home, you can place it into the designated section. If your product can be sold to companies, place the product into a special section.

Once your business grows, you may have so many products or services you can offer specific catalogs for each one. For example, a mail-order lighting manufacturer sold many lamps to different businesses, including hospitals all over the country. They decided to develop a special catalog called "Medical Lighting Catalog" and mailed it to all the hospitals and hospital-equipment dealers in the country. This led to an entirely new sales division for the company and a very profitable market, because the company discovered a new vehicle to reach their market.

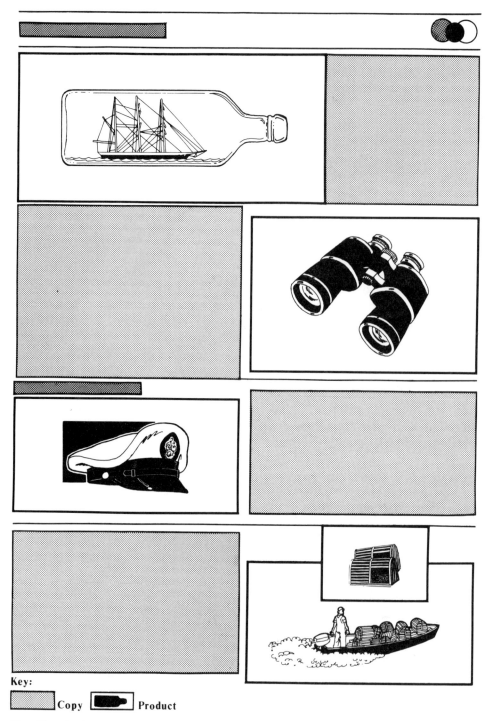

Key:

[Copy]   [Product]

Fig. 16-1. In the copy block method, you simply show your product and then write hard-hitting copy to be placed next to the illustration, describing the benefits and features.

THE COVER IS ESSENTIAL

The cover grabs the prospect's attention right away. You never get a second chance to make a favorable first impression. Make your cover stand out so your reader will take the necessary time to read it. Spend time to produce a cover that will work for you.

KNOW YOUR CUSTOMER'S SPECIFIC NEEDS

A catalog offering products and services to the purchasing agents is much different than a catalog offered to your customers. The professional buyer looks for quantity discounts, quality specifications, specific shipping costs, warranties, return policies, and all the other information so essential to them. Many purchasing agents keep catalogs on file. You might want to produce your catalog punched for a three ring binder, so the customer can file it away easily.

Consider sending your catalog to stores: food stores, department stores, book stores. Send your catalog to people who want and need your product. For example, a large ceramic supply mail-order company sends out their catalog on a regular basis to ceramic makers, to offer them new ceramic ideas. Their customers purchase their ceramic supplies, including brushes, molds, tools, and stains, right out of the catalog. Some of their customers use the new ceramic ideas to teach their students. The key concept here is to send your catalog to the most interested people—those who understand and can benefit with your product.

KEEP NEW IDEAS AND PROFITABLE ITEMS IN THE FRONT

A good catalog not only offers new and exciting ideas, but presents special offers throughout to keep the reader interested enough to continue to read the complete catalog. When you use a specific selling point, such as free shipping for an order over $100, continue to remind the customers or readers about this throughout the catalog. Feature your most important and profitable products in the beginning of the catalog; studies show that the first few pages of a catalog are the most read. Some mail-order people fail to put their most important products in the beginning of their catalog and find their results are poor, reflecting their poor catalog organization.

CONSIDER USING ADDITIONAL ORDER FORMS

Direct your reader to where the order form is located in the catalog and where additional order forms can be found. The extra order forms makes reordering much easier, and permit your customer to send the catalog and order forms to their friends and associates. Some mail-order companies ask their customers if they need additional order forms, and will send them free of charge. Make it easy for your customers to order from you.

CATALOG COPY MUST DISCUSS CUSTOMER BENEFITS

The reader of your catalog wants to know how the product will benefit him or her once the decision to buy is completed. Will the product increase his or her income? Will it save time and money? Will the product increase his or her popularity with others? Will the product make the customer more attractive to the opposite sex? Review the copy techniques discussed in Chapter 5 when you develop the catalog. Stress the benefits to your catalog reader. For example, tell your reader about the safety features of your products. Discuss all the important features, to get your reader to order from you.

MAKE YOUR COPY EASY TO UNDERSTAND

Make your sentences short and clear. Never overestimate the customer's ability to understand your message. Keep the copy simple. Strive for complete understanding. Use words that people understand. Use words that motivate the reader to action. Your job will be to convince the portion of the readers who are ready to order now. One mail-order owner makes a practice of writing the copy for the catalog, and then asking his twelve-year-old son to read it. Once he determines that his son understands the copy, he uses it in the final catalog.

STRESS YOUR GUARANTEE OR OTHER ATTRACTIVE FEATURES

One mail-order owner from New York offered a free trial offer for his products, but failed to mention this important element in his catalog. When you have an unconditional guarantee on your products, make this important point in your copy. Some mail-order catalogs state their guarantee on numerous pages of the catalog. State the points necessary to gain your readers confidence. Move the reader through the decision-making process. Once the reader feels your product can benefit him or her, and you offer a guarantee, the ordering process is much easier.

MAKE YOUR CATALOG PAY OFF FOR YOU

By the time you start your catalog, you have information from advertisements you placed, and from sales letters and direct-mail material you have used. What advertisement or material worked for you? Which testimonials? Keep this information in mind when you put your catalog together. For example, one successful mail-order owner uses his best print advertisements in his catalog. Use your best ideas and results in your catalog. As the owner of a catalog, you must be very strict about the products or services you choose to display in your catalog. For example, if product A is not pulling in your catalog month after month, you might want to replace it with another product that will pull better for you. Just like the publisher who charges you to run a classified or display advertisement in a magazine, you must also monitor very carefully. For example, in the table below, you will find one method to monitor the products in your catalog.

When a product begins to lose sales, try to determine the reason for it. Are you giving the product enough exposure? Do you feature the product in the right section of the catalog? Do you offer the reader enough benefits to purchase your product? Make an effort to keep your products selling. When all else fails, replace the product with one that will sell for you.

Catalog Monitoring

	Units Sold	Total Sales
Product A	100	$2,999
Product B	75	4,230
Product C	20	120
Product F	125	1,125

WATCH THE POSTAL COSTS

Take your eight-page catalog to the post office, and get a price on the cost to mail it for both first-class mail and bulk mail. Some mail-order owners make the mistake of weighing and pricing the cost of mailing after the catalog is printed.

DO YOU NEED FOUR-COLOR CATALOGS?

Four-color catalogs are great—when you can afford them. In the beginning of your business, I recommend that you use a black-and-white catalog. Another option, you could use colored paper to give your catalog a two-color dimension. Keep a file of catalogs you receive in your regular mail, and send for catalogs to get various ideas.

HOW MANY COPIES SHOULD YOU PRINT?

Print enough copies that you expect to use while maintaining the same prices. The more copies you purchase, the lower the price per copy. If you buy 10,000 copies, your total cost would be lower than if you purchase 40,000 copies, but when you run out of the 10,000, you will need to reorder more. Order the amount you need, but make certain you receive an estimate for 5,000, 10,000, 20,000, 30,000, 40,000, and 50,000 copies.

OFFER SPECIALS

Good catalogs offer products or services in an exciting manner. A catalog sets a mood. A catalog keeps the reader's interest in mind: every reader is looking for value and you can offer specials to motivate the reader to order. When a product is new, feature it in your catalog. It is only new once. Good catalogs are designed so that reading them is fun. Each page is exciting, containing one interesting product or service after another.

If you offer a special, with an attractive price for the value offered, your reader is more likely to decide to buy that product, and then buy additional products at the same time. Your customer is looking for the little extra before he buys. By offering specials, you are offering recommendations to your customer. Your customer depends on you to offer the best products or services in the most exciting manner possible.

REFER TO DIFFERENT PARTS OF THE CATALOG

Move the reader to other parts of the catalog to offer additional information. For example, one mail-order catalog states on the bottom of a page on calculators, "See pages 7 and 8 for complete specifications, solution books, and accessory information." A good catalog also asks for the order. Tell your reader where the order page is located, and how easy it is to order. Make the ordering process as easy as possible to increase your catalog orders.

STRIVE FOR A PROFESSIONAL APPEARANCE

Your catalog is an extension of you and your business. It must look professional to succeed. It must be organized, easy to read and understand, and direct your customer to the order page. Your catalog is another member of your printing family, which includes your sales letter, brochure, order card, envelopes, and other printed material. Make certain your catalog looks as polished as possible. Review the catalog of a New Hampshire mail-order dealer of sewing kits in Fig. 16-2.

WHAT IS THE BEST TIME TO MAIL YOUR CATALOGS?

Many mailers will send their catalogs in late September or early October so that their customers can take their time and choose some of the products for Christmas gifts. The catalog method of selling is an excellent way to reach an intense group of potential customers. Catalog customers will spend hours of their time looking over the many products you have to offer. They want time to pick just the right product. They will list on the order card the size of the product, the color, and the quantity. Send your catalog at least once a year—twice a year is even better.

Many gift shops have used the catalog method of selling for a number of years, and have sold many millions of dollars worth of jewelry, planters, clocks, mailboxes, glassware, furniture, clothing, lamps, shoes, boots, sculptures, paperweights, and placemats. The professional in mail order will replace slow-moving products with new products. Make certain that your catalog is printed professionally and the paper used is of good quality. Many catalog buyers will judge the quality of your products simply by the "look" of your catalog and accompanying literature.

There's a little town in New Hampshire in which mail order is earning a nice living for two middle-aged women. They have their house converted to conduct a very successful mail-order business. They also converted their garage into a receiving and shipping area for their business. They select numerous products with a very New England style to them; for example, many sea and nautical items, and other unique gifts that will appeal to people living in various parts of the United States. They mail their catalog twice a year, in the fall and spring, to feature products used at these times, including furniture and clothing. They use their own list, because they find that this pulls in orders better than any other list. They continue to rent lists to help them sell more products. They talk to a number of sales people to get ideas about even better products for their customers. When a product begins to slow down in sales, they look for a replacement for that space on the catalog. They know that space is valuable and must be used to pay for itself.

You also must feel the same way in your mail-order business. Use all available space on your direct-mail package or your catalog, with a careful eye on your return on investment. The business took years to build to a successful business, but now their customers look to them as friends that send us some nice ideas twice a year in the form of an easy-to-read and understandable catalog.

ALLOW ENOUGH TIME TO DO IT PROPERLY

Many mail-order owners get excited once they decided to include a catalog for their business. They want the catalog right away. Anything worthwhile takes time. Allow yourself the time necessary to do it right. Set up a time frame with your printer for each step in the process, from typesetting to printing. By rushing the printer, you will upset your relationship and jeopardize the success of your project. Give sufficient time for the ink to dry. One mail-order owner from New York was so excited about sending out his catalog, he picked up the catalog immediately, and since the ink was not fully dried, the ink was smudged. Many of his catalogs were ruined.

Now let's summarize this chapter.

SUMMARY OF KEY POINTS

- A catalog might be eight pages in the beginning of your business and grow to 99 pages when your business can support it.
- The advantage to the catalog is that the buyer can keep your catalog on file, or in the office, or coffee table, and then buy from you later.

Continued on p. 190.

Polarfleece® Bunting Pullover

Snuggle into this stylish and warm pullover sewn from Polarfleece® bunting fabric. Lightweight, breathable, and machine washable.

Colors: silver, charcoal or navy; with navy knit trim.

Price $27.95 . . . . **Men's XL $29.95**

Women	Men	Chest	Length	Item No.
XS		31-32	24	P29E
S	XS	33-34	25	P29F
M	S	35-36	26	P29S
L	M	37-40	27	P29M
XL	L	41-44	28	P29L
	XL	45-48	29	P29X

Polarfleece® Bunting Jacket

OUR EASIEST GARMENT

Our easiest jacket to sew is warm, soft and easy to care for. The navy stretch-knit waistband and cuffs are attractive trim and, with the raglan sleeves, ensure a comfortable fit. The polyester Polarfleece® fabric is lightweight, breathable, machine washable, quick drying and warmer than wool — even when wet.

Colors: silver, charcoal or navy; with navy knit trim.

Price $27.95 . . . . **Men's XL $29.95**

Women	Men	Chest	Length	Item No.
XS		31-32	24	P27E
S	XS	33-34	25	P27F
M	S	35-36	26	P27S
L	M	37-40	27	P27M
XL	L	41-44	28	P27L
	XL	45-48	29	P27X

Highlander Pullover

Tough Expedition Cloth for durability & s-t-r-e-t-c-h knit for a perfect fit...

Our sporty Pullover is breathable, lightweight, and packs easily. Tightly woven 65% polyester / 35% cotton Expedition Cloth resists wind and rain, and the double-layer nylon knit collar, waistband and cuffs ensure a comfortable fit. A roomy raglan shoulder, a zippered "kangaroo"' cargo pouch and tunnel pocket for hand warming make this a versatile garment for outdoor activities. Machine washable.

Colors: red, forest green, silver or navy; with navy trim.

Price $26.95 . . . . **Men's XL $28.95**

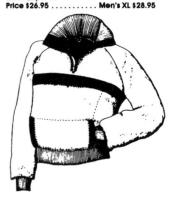

Women	Men	Chest	Length	Item No.
XS		31-32	26½	P35E
S	XS	33-34	27	P35F
M	S	35-36	27	P35S
L	M	37-40	27½	P35M
XL	L	41-44	28½	P35L
	XL	45-48	30	P35X

Snappy Jacket

This versatile jacket is easy to sew because there are no zippers and we pre-set the snaps. The tightly woven 65% polyester / 35% cotton Expedition Cloth makes this an ideal wind breaker that

NEW

also resists the rain. A perfect fit is ensured by the nylon knit collar, waistband and cuffs. Machine washable.

Colors: red, forest green, silver or navy; with navy trim.

Price: $26.95 . . . . **Men's XL $28.95**

Women	Men	Chest	Length	Item No.
XS		31-32	26½	P37E
S	XS	33-34	27	P37F
M	S	35-36	27	P37S
L	M	37-40	27½	P37M
XL	L	41-44	28½	P37L
	XL	45-48	30	P37X

Included in your TimberLine Sewing Kit is precision pre-cut fabric notched for easy match up and construction, insulation (where necessary), plenty of color-matching thread, notions, and easily followed instructions.

Fig. 16-2. Design your catalog based on the product or service you are selling. In this catalog, the owner sells sewing kits and features quality and style. His business allows customers to save money because they make the items themselves.

SHIP TO: DATE _____

NAME _____

ADDRESS _____

_____

CITY _____ STATE _____ ZIP _____

Telephone Number-Area Code _____ Number _____

For Fast Service

To place VISA or MasterCard orders, call (603) 435-8888 weekdays 8 a.m. - 5 p.m., or leave a message on the phone recorder anytime (no collect calls please).

QUANT	ITEM NUMBER	SIZE	COLOR 1st CHOICE	COLOR 2nd CHOICE	DESCRIPTION	PRICE EACH	TOTAL PRICE
	CATALOGS FOR YOUR FRIENDS					FREE	

MasterCard VISA

☐ Check or money order
☐ Master Card
☐ VISA (Bank Americard)

Card Account Number

Credit Card Expiration Date

Master Card 4 digit number over name

Customer Signature _____

TOTAL	
Shipping Handling & Insurance SEE TABLE BELOW	
Air delivery within U.S. $5.00 extra (up to 5 lbs.)	
GRAND TOTAL	

We ship U.P.S.

✂ -

Ordering

For fast service you can place your MasterCard or VISA orders by calling (603) 435-8888 (sorry, but we cannot accept collect calls). You can also order by using the enclosed order blank or by writing us giving full details.

We invite you to visit our factory outlet on Clark St. (near the town swimming pool) in Pittsfield, N.H. Our hours are Monday through Friday 8 a.m. to 5 p.m., year round; Saturdays 9 a.m. to 12 noon, September through May.

Payment: Please send check or money order in U.S. funds. We also honor MasterCard or VISA. Please make sure to include your card number and expiration date on any orders. No C.O.D. orders accepted.

Choosing Your Size

Refer to the measurements listed in the description section of each item and select the size that most closely matches your measurements. Sleeves and most body lengths can be shortened during construction.
Chest: Measure fullest part of chest.
Sleeve length: Measure from point (A) to wrist (B). Elbow must be bent as shown.
Body length: Measure from point (A) to (C) or (D).

If you have any questions on obtaining the proper size, supply us with details on your height, weight, chest, sleeve length, hip, and dress or sport coat size, and we will send you the correct size kit. Also advise us if you prefer a tight, medium or loose fit.

Shipping

U.S. Shipments: Shipments are sent via United Parcel Service where possible unless Parcel Post is requested. Please give us a street address. Add $5.00 to air shipments within the U.S.A. on orders up to 5 lbs. Orders over 5 lbs. will be charged at U.P.S. or U.S. Postal Service rates plus $1.00 handling.

Canadian Shipments: Orders are payable in U.S. funds. Add $5.00 extra to each order, which will be sent Parcel Post. Any Customs Duty is your responsibility.

We ship most orders within 24 hours.

SHIPPING, HANDLING, INSURANCE Order Amount	Shipping Rate
under $20	$2.50
$20 to $75	$3.50
over $75	$4.50

Discount

A 10% educational discount off all regular prices is given on each group order over $50 delivered to a single address. Schools, clubs, and many other organizations qualify for this 10% group discount. Discounts do not apply to "specials", sale items, or raw materials.

Raw Materials

We sell nylon fabrics by the yard. Down insulation and notions are also available. A materials list will be sent upon request, and a fabric swatch card may be purchased for $3.00.

Guarantee

Your good will is important to us and we guarantee your complete satisfaction with each kit. If for any reason you are not satisfied, return the kit with proof of purchase and reason for dissatisfaction and we will refund your money or exchange it, whichever you prefer.
Before, during or after assembly you can return a TimberLine sewing kit.

TimberLine sewing kits

We invite you to visit our factory outlet on Clark Street in Pittsfield, NH
Open Monday–Friday, 8 a.m.–5 p.m. year-round; Saturday 9 a.m.–Noon, September through May.

Fig. 16-2. Continued.

- Your carefully planned catalog sent out to the right list can expand your business.
- A catalog requires planning time.
- Develop a theme with your customers' needs, and join them together.
- The cover is important because it can get the customers' attention.
- Put your new ideas and products in the front of your catalog.
- Use additional order forms.
- Use your advertising experience in your catalog.
- Typesetting can save you time and money.
- Watch your postal costs.
- Start with black-and-white printed catalogs.
- Print the correct number of catalogs, based on what you need during the next six months to a year.
- Offer specials—everyone enjoys a good deal.
- Refer to the different parts of the catalog.
- Allow enough time to do it properly.

17

The Full Campaign

DURING THE PAST SEVERAL CHAPTERS, WE HAVE DISCUSSED VARIOUS PRINCIPLES to make your mail-order business succeed. We have discussed everything from choosing a product to selecting a market and writing the advertisement. All of these principles must work together to make your business work. When you do one without the others, limited success will result. Each component must be well thought out, planned, organized, and then implemented in order to work on your behalf. Be sure to present your message in the most forceful manner. A well-developed campaign will do this for you. Consider, for example, the political campaign. A good politician tries to determine his or her best strengths and then presents them to the people based on the issues of the day. Politicians stress what they can do for people and downplay their weaknesses. In a similar manner, you take your product or service, and then develop your promotional strategy based on the way you want your product positioned. *Positioning* refers to the way you want your consumers to view or see your product. When I develop a campaign for my manuals and books in mail order, I position them as the best books on the market, to help them earn more money at work or in the business. A mail-order owner of toys positions her toys as the safest and best wooden toys available today.

POSITIONING IS ESSENTIAL

Your mail-order campaign is only as good as the way you see yourself in your business. This image must be communicated to your market. Large companies use positioning to help them get their message across. For example, a large national company selling razor blades likes to position their razor blades as the best product on the market with a good price. Their campaign stressed this positioning strategy in all advertisements and promotional efforts.

Positioning has a great deal to do with the reasons you started a mail-order business in the first place. If you review your basic reasons for starting your business, you will determine an excellent way to position your product. For example, a recently retired woman from Wisconsin had pets all her life and wanted to devote more time to this interest in her retirement. She plans to sell pet toys, books, and even a newsletter on pets to her customers. She wants to sell products and services that will help her customers enjoy their pets more. Her positioning strategy should be a company with the main interest of bringing people closer to their pets.

YOUR THEME TIES THE CAMPAIGN TOGETHER

Your theme is a specific subject to set your campaign apart from others. Your theme might be "Products to Help You Lose Weight and Feel Better" or "Products to Save You Time and Money." The theme can be tied directly to your positioning strategy of trying to help your customer look more attractive, get the job, or start an exercise program. The theme is the heavy twine that can tie the campaign elements tightly together into an understandable, benefits-filled, hard-hitting campaign.

Your campaign theme must be something your customers can understand easily. Connect with your customer by a direct theme. Themes are with you from the moment you wake in the morning until you fall asleep at night. The oil company has a campaign on how they try to take environmental factors into consideration while drilling for oil. The forestry company informs you of the new trees they plant to replace the trees cut each day. Other companies focus their campaign on their large purchases of products to give you the best price. Churches and schools also employ themes to reach people more effectively.

For example, I worked for a large business-education company with schools in major cities all over the country. We developed a theme to try to get the students to attend school regularly, graduate, and then attain a full-time job, and eventually a career. We picked a theme called "See You Tomorrow" with the basic strategy of getting the student to take one day at a time, and attend school each day. Regular attendance was needed to make it to the final requirements: tests and, finally, graduation. This "See You Tomorrow" theme was supported by management. Prizes given to the students with the best attendance records and some genuine attention was paid to the students. Banners showing the theme were hung in the school, and the faculty and staff joined in to support the theme. We made it a success because we supported the theme each day. A theme will not work for you unless you make a daily and concentrated effort to make your campaign a success. In short, you must keep selling. Your mail-order business will succeed when you keep selling your products and services on a regular basis.

SELLING IN MAIL ORDER IS ALMOST EVERYTHING

Sometimes my students choose mail order because they feel that, since they deal with the customer by mail and never see the customer face-to-face, there is very little selling involved. This is incorrect. Selling is the single most important thing you do on a daily basis in mail order. You sell with your offer, your sales letter, your campaign, and your classified or display ads. You sell with your knowledge of your product or service and your understanding of the customer and the customer's needs and desires. The difference between selling for the ABC company and selling in your own mail-order business is the lack of chain of command. You are not required to report to someone for your sales record. You have the responsibility of setting a goal for your sales, and then working hard to reach it. Mail-order selling is just as difficult as any other selling. In some ways more difficult, because the customer is difficult to sell, especially from an advertisement or a sales letter. Good selling requires listening to the customer and offering the customer just what is needed to reach a satisfied agreement. Keep your sales skills sharp to succeed. In order to get to know more about the skills and personality traits necessary, I offer you the following piece written by an anonymous author.

What is a Salesperson?

A salesperson is a pin on a map to the sales manager, a quota to the factory, an overloaded expense account to the auditor, a bookkeeping item called "cost-of-selling" to the treasurer, a smile and a wisecrack to the receptionist, and a purveyor of flattery to the buyer.

A salesperson needs the endurance of Hercules, the brass of Barnum, the craft of Machiavelli, the tact of a diplomat, the tongue of an orator, the charm of a playboy, and the brain of a computer.

He or she must be impervious to insult, indifference, anger, scorn, complaint, and be razor-sharp even after drinking until dawn with a customer.

He or she must have the stamina to sell all day, entertain all evening, drive all night to the next town, and be on the job fresh at 9 A.M.

He or she must be good at story-telling and willing to lose at golf and cards.

He or she wishes the merchandise was better, the prices lower, the commissions higher, the territory smaller, the competitors more ethical, the goods more promptly delivered, the boss more sympathetic, the advertising more effective and the customers more human.

But he or she is an optimist, so he makes the sale anyway.

He or she lives or dies by the daily report.

He or she rolls his days away in a tedium of planes, trains and cars. He or she sleeps the night away in cheerless hotel rooms.

Each morning he or she hoists onto his back the dead weight of last year's sales record and this year's quota and goes forth to do it all over again.

Yet, for all that, he or she is absolutely certain that tomorrow will be better and there is nothing he would rather do, anybody he would rather be—than a salesman.

—ANONYMOUS

This piece best describes the important role of the salesperson in any business, and especially in the mail-order business. Each day, you should try to ask yourself: What did I sell today? Mail-order success is measured in enough sales to make a profit, so you can continue to expand. You are your own boss, so sell, and keep selling to succeed.

YOUR CAMPAIGN IS ALL YEAR LONG

Unless you sell a very seasonal product like Christmas trees, you must plan to keep selling your product or service all year long to earn your profits. Even if you sell toys, Christmas in not your only season. Keep your campaign a year-long process. Mail order was once viewed as a seasonal business, with the bulk of the sales in the winter months. People buy products and services all year long. Your job is to develop a campaign that will continue to interest customers over and over again, so they will continue to buy from you.

SHOULD YOU CHANGE YOUR CAMPAIGN THEME?

Give your campaign theme a chance to succeed. You cannot test it correctly until you run it for at least six months or one year. If you find that the inquiries and sales are not coming in strong enough, you can consider changing or adjusting your campaign theme. For example, Nicole F., a mail-order owner from Mississippi who sells sewing kits, used a theme to save money for one year. It worked fine, but later, the sales slowed, and she changed it to play up the fun and satisfaction the buyers would receive by making their own clothes.

Keep your campaign theme for a year. Good campaign themes will work in the cold days of January, the snowy days of February, the windy March days, the rainy April afternoons, the sunny May mornings, the airy June days, the hot July evenings, the humid August days, the fallish September days, the Indian summer days of October, the chilly mornings in November, and the brisk days of December. A good campaign theme will have trouble with some months, but will ultimately win the war.

Magazines use their campaign theme to keep their readers interested and satisfied. For example, just before the Christmas holidays, they choose articles for their readers that deal with this holiday. You can also select articles and features that deal with the spring, summer, fall, and winter seasons, or break it down further into months of the year. For example, a business magazine developed a campaign theme of ''Turning Your Business into Profit,'' and each month deals with a different facet of the theme.

January—New Sales Techniques

February—Production Improvements

March—Watching Energy Costs

April—Employee Costs

May—Employee Benefits and Programs

June—Temporary Help Ideas

July—Advertising Ideas

August—Using Consultants Successfully

September—Direct Mail

October—Telemarketing

November—Reading Profit Reports

December—Planning for Better Profits

You can adopt this idea to your mail-order business. Each month, your advertisement can focus on a product or service for that month. Keep that campaign going and stay with that theme, it will work for you if sufficient time is given to it.

HOW MUCH MONEY DO YOU NEED TO START?

You need at least $400 minimum to run your first advertisement and print up some sales material to use the two-step method. Once your business starts, expect to spend at least 20 percent of your total sales on advertising, such as classified or display advertisements. Turn your money from sales right back into the business for more advertisements and printing material.

YOU MUST WORK ON YOUR BUSINESS EACH DAY

Successful mail-order people keep their mail-order business going strong by continuing to do all the things necessary to keep it going. You never finish anything until you start it. You will never receive the orders until you send out the information to your inquiries. Do something each day. By working on your business every day, you keep your momentum going.

109 STEPS TO THE FULL CAMPAIGN

The full campaign means putting it all together. It means going over all the reasons why you can make your business succeed, and then achieving success. Review this full campaign often, and be willing to self-correct to get your business back on track.

Setting Up Your Home Office

1. Choose an area to give yourself privacy.
2. Use a section of a room if necessary.
3. Spend time daily in your home office.
4. Check with your local town or city clerk for licenses and zoning requirements of your area.
5. Give family members a chance to help you.

Your Company

6. Choose a name that is easy to remember, but communicates your products or services to the customer.
7. A name like ''Supreme Office Supply Products Company'' gets the point across.
8. Use your complete street address, such as 670 River Road, Plarytown, Massachusetts, rather than using a post office box number.
9. Choose a sole proprietorship, partnership, or corporation for your company.
10. Your company will develop a personality of its own. Make an effort to develop the best possible image.

Product Selection

11. Choose your product or service carefully.
12. Choose a product that you enjoy and know well.
13. Your product should be unique and practical—one that can be sold over and over.
14. Choose a product people use up and have to reorder from you.
15. Keep a product ideas file.
16. Start with a lead product, and then build a line of products.
17. Become known as the mail-order owner who features this particular line of products.
18. Watch for changes in public interests, and keep offering products to meet the times.

Suppliers

19. Try to be your own supplier. Produce the product or service on your own.
20. The best suppliers are found at trade shows, gift shows, and by recommendations from other mail-order owners.

21. Make small orders with your supplier before you sign a long-term contract with a set price.
22. The supplier is in business just like you.
23. Make certain your product supplier can deliver.
24. Match the product to your market. Sell gifts to known gift buyers.

Finding the Customer

25. The market is the group of potential customers with desire to buy your product.
26. Your market might be teachers, banks, sports fans, antique buyers, or self-help book buyers.
27. Determine the demographics and psychographics of your market.
28. Hit your target market directly.
29. Review the Mail-Order Bill of Rights.
30. Sell to other successful mail-order owners.
31. The government offers free secondary research sources.
32. Find your market, then communicate. Build up a relationship to keep your share of the market.

Write Copy That Sells

33. Get to know your product or service.
34. Get the reader excited about the benefits of the product.
35. Use the AIDA approach.
36. Use simple, easy-to-understand words.
37. Try a personal approach to persuade the customer to buy from you.
38. Start with a good headline, and follow your sales promotion to the end.
39. Remember to ask for the order.
40. Read your copy as a customer before you use it.

Advertising

41. Choose magazines that segment your market.
42. Classified advertising builds your house list.
43. Magazines have 2 to 3 months closing times.
44. Magazines offer longer life than newspapers, as well as intense readership.
45. News releases give you *free* advertising.
46. Send out 50 to 100 copies of your news release to magazines, newspapers, associations, and newsletters.
47. Keep testing magazines and advertisements until you get a winner.
48. Regular advertising is the engine in your business.
49. Advertising does not cost you; it pays for you.
50. State the reasons why your product is better.
51. Make your claims, and then back them up.

52. Key your advertising to determine what magazines are pulling the orders for you.
53. Your advertising program is an important part of your full campaign.

Your Sales Material

54. Professional sales material sells.
55. Misspellings, smudges, and black dots will hurt your image.
56. Essential elements include a sales letter, brochure, order card, and reply envelope.
57. Your sales material is your opportunity to tell your full story.
58. Get a quotation from 3 to 4 printers.
59. Some sales materials can be prepared on your personal computer.
60. Do one printing project at a time.
61. Give the printer enough time to finish the job.

Customer Service

62. Show customers they count.
63. Mail-order success equals satisfied customers.
64. Good customer service promotes a positive company's image.
65. Handle complaints as quickly as possible.
66. Delay with angry customers in mail order means complaints to local, state, and federal officials.
67. If you state shipment within 48 hours of the order, make sure you do it.
68. Satisfied customers add to your profits.
69. Set up a system to handle inquiries from potential customers.
70. Good customer service motivates a prospect into becoming a customer.
71. Turn a customer into a long-term customer.
72. Professional customer service turns a new customer into a heavy user.
73. L.L. Bean grew to one of the biggest mail-order companies by offering individualized service for every customer.

Sales Promotion

74. Use the lost leader approach.
75. Sell the lead product and sell your full line.
76. Follow up new customers with new offers.
77. Offer premiums or special discounts occasionally. Don't give your product away.
78. Try offering free information or booklets to promote more sales.
79. Continue to stress the value of your product or service rather than any premium.

80. The best sales promotion is managing your business and giving the best service possible to get the customer to buy again.

Your Offer

81. Your offer includes your full terms, price, product/service description, guarantees, bonuses, and ordering instructions.
82. Make your offer easy to understand.
83. Get your customer involved with the offer.
84. To get the order, give your customer the best possible offer.
85. Consider a free trial offer.
86. Once you find an offer that works, continue it until it stops working.

Mailing Lists

87. Select carefully. Many lists are over-worked.
88. Test a list of 1,000 to 2,000 names if possible.
89. Once a list works for you, keep using it.
90. Use a list broker.
91. For extra revenue, rent your house list when you are established.
92. Keep your list clean and updated.

Managing Your Business

93. Management means knowing the cost per inquiry, unit cost per product, all expenses, and profits or losses.
94. Test important things. Avoid the trivial.
95. Test lists, mailing packages, offers, and magazines.
96. Do a profit and loss on each advertisement or mailing.

Legalities

97. Avoid lotteries and obscene literature.
98. Ship mail-order products or services within (30) thirty days.
99. Deliver on your claims and promises in your ads and literature.
100. Keep good records of your sales and expenses.

Final Word

101. Keep your product quality high.
102. Advertise all-year-round.
103. Keep improving in your service to the customer.
104. You learn the business by doing it.
105. Test important elements of your business regularly.
106. Make changes when necessary. Never make changes when things are working well.
107. Treat everyone fairly, including customers, employees, suppliers, printers, and other mail-order companies.
108. Smile and act like a winner. Everything you do will reflect it.
109. Good luck.

Appendix A

Most Commonly Asked Questions

Q. How do I get started?

A. Good question. Many of my mail-order seminar attendees ask this question to themselves and to me privately after the seminar is over. You cannot start unless you set a deadline. Do one thing at a time. Once completed, go to the next activity; finish No. 1 before you go to No. 2. Below you will find a set of mail-order activities you must complete to get started. Set a time limit on No. 1 and get started on it. Once you finish it, check it off and go to No. 2. Use this system to get started successfully.

Check when
finished

_____	1. Select product/service, i.e. Jan 1, 19__
_____	2. Select target market
_____	3. Prepare classified ad
_____	4. Place classified ad
_____	5. Order products/services
_____	6. Prepare sales literature
_____	7. Prepare for advertisement appearance
_____	8. Set up an inquiry fulfillment system
_____	9. Schedule regular advertising
_____	10. Develop management techniques
_____	11. Review the business regularly
_____	12. Develop a campaign for next year

Q. *How important are computer skills in starting my mail-order business at home?*

A. All skills are important. Computer skills can be very helpful in your business to save time and effort. It is possible to run your business without the computer skills, but the more information you have, the better decisions you can make in your business.

Q. *If I decide on a computer for the mail-order business, how do I pick one?*

A. A computer is not essential, but it can be a worthwhile tool. Many mail-order people use a computer to save time and effort. A computer can help you keep your list updated and prepare sales material. It can keep track of sales, costs, profits, losses, customer purchases and returns, mail-order tests, and reports. If you plan to purchase a home or personal computer, consider the number and the variety of jobs for which you expect to use it. The more you use the computer, the better chance you will get your investment returned to you.

Shop carefully for your computer. It is similar to buying a car. Shop at various stores and compare various models and manufacturers. Have an idea about how you want to use the computer, for example, for word processing. Ask about the store's service policies, and get the full details on the warranty. Write down the service and warranty for each manufacturer. What are their training policies? How long is the training? Make certain you take the necessary training to use the computer properly.

You should also have a basic understanding of the essential parts of the computer.

Central Processing Unit. The Central Processing Unit is the "brains" of the computer. The CPU takes instruction and stores it away for later use. When you want to recall the data, you use the keyboard to instruct the computer to follow what has been recorded on the microprocessor. The CPU is also called the *hardware* of the computer system.

Software. These are the programs that inform the computer what to do. They are contained on "floppy" disks. There are many programs available for record keeping, accounting, text-editing, financial analysis, and educational programs. Ask about the programs to use in your mail-order business, such as list maintenance and records of customers. Examine the software carefully before you buy the computer.

Disk Drive. With this feature you can record stored information from disks almost immediately. Some computers have one or two disk drives built right into the system.

The Printer. This is a large typewriter, usually on a stand, that prints the material the computer retrieves onto paper for a "hard" copy. There are three types of printers: the *dot matrix printer*, which forms letters, numbers, and images with tiny dots (a letter-quality printer is a sophisticated type of dot matrix printer that produces letters with high resolution); the *daisy-wheel* *printer*, which is a single-strike printer that prints letters on the paper with the same quality of a good electric typewriter; and the *laser printer*, a very high-resolution printer that uses laser beams to create its images. You should note, however, that letter-quality and laser printers are very expensive and, at the beginning stages of your business, will probably not be worth the expense.

Final Word. Your computer system is only as good as the quality of information fed into it. The person running the computer must be careful to handle and process the data correctly, and run the system accurately. The computer is a multiuse tool—the more you use it, the more you will realize from your investment.

Q. *What is the most important thing to remember in a mail-order business?*
A. Consistency. Do things right, and keep doing them. Pick good products and services. Run advertisements regularly. Write material that gets opened and read. Give good service. Keep selling.

Q. *What federal tax forms are required to run a mail-order business?*
A. If you plan to hire help with your sole proprietorship, or you want to start a partnership or corporation, you need an employer identification number. Contact the Internal Revenue Service and ask for Form SS-4.

Sole proprietorships must file annually:
   a. Federal Income Tax.
      —Form 1040
      —Federal Schedule C (Profit and Loss)
      —Federal Schedule SE (self)
   b. State Income Tax. This varies state by state, check with your local state tax department.
   c. Check with your accountant if you have any questions on accounting or records for your business.

Q. *Any final advice on being successful?*
A. Yes, there are just 5 things that are essential.
   1. Sell quality products/services.
   2. Know your customers well.
   3. Keep testing.
   4. Keep up with the changes in the mail-order field.
   5. Action speaks louder than words, do the work to succeed.

Q. *What is the best-possible direct-mail format or package?*
A. Try to sell one product only, and include a good sales letter with many benefits and reasons why the prospect should buy from you. You will find a rough letter and a finished letter on pages 96 – 97 and 102 – 105. Include with the sales letter a good reply card that summarizes the offer (see example on page 106) and a brochure that shows the product in use or highlights different aspects of the product from the sales letter. This package is very impor-

tant to your success in mail order; it will be your follow-up mailing for your inquiries to your classified ad, and it can be your basic mailing for your direct-mail campaign. Once you get a direct-mail package that works, keep using it until you reach the point of diminishing returns.

Q. *In the book you discussed various media, magazines, newspapers, radio, and even specialty advertising. Which one is the best one for me? I'll be honest, I don't know, and I am confused about the best one to sell my product or service.*

A. Excellent question. I enjoy your honesty. In mail order, the best medium is the magazine because it gives you long life, and it can reach directly to your target market. For example, if you wanted to reach fire fighters, you can run an advertisement in the *Firefighter Magazine*. A good advertisement in a well-read magazine will increase inquiries, which will build your mailing list. You can then sell your customers other offers, and then put together a catalog to sell them all year long.

Radio and television can sell mail-order products, but the cost is often too high in the beginning of your business. Once you get established, you can experiment with different media and build your list and reputation.

Appendix B

Resources for Your Business

Mail Order Association

Direct Marketing Assoc.
6 E. 43rd St.
New York, NY 10017

Comment: Offers mail-order marketing information. Includes free weekly newspapers, seminars, publications. Also includes educational foundations and runs seminars, workshops and programs.

Advertising Services

Standard Rate and Data Service Inc.
3004 Glenview Rd.
Wilmette, IL 60091

Comment: Provides all the information you need to place your advertisements in the best possible publications and outlets.

Government Sponsored Resources

SCORE
Service Corps of Retired Executives
U.S. Small Business Administration
National Office
1129 20th St. N.W. Suite 410
Washington, DC 20416
(202) 653-6279

Comment: Offers free counseling for small businesses by retired executives with knowledge and experience in the field. Also offers seminars and workshops. Contact your local office.

Small Business Development Centers

Office of Chief Counsel for Advocacy
Small Business Administration
1441 L St., N.W.
Washington, DC 20416
(202) 653-7561 (in Washington, DC)
(800) 368-5855

Comment: The Small Business Administration offers management and technical advice to existing and prospective small businesses. SBDC combines the federal, state and local resources to give small businesses what they need to succeed. These centers are located in colleges and universities.

Small Business Answer Desk

Office of the Chief Counsel for Advocacy
Small Business Administration
1441 L St., N.W.
Washington, DC 20416
(202) 653-7561 (in Washington, DC)
(800) 368-5855

Comment: The Small Business Administration's Office of Advocacy has set up a special telephone number to answer calls on a toll free hotline.

Chamber of Commerce USA
1615 H St., N.W.
Washington, DC 20062
(202) 659-6000

Comment: The Chamber of Commerce has available numerous publications on small businesses.

Government Publications

Superintendent of Documents
U.S. Government Printing Office
Washington, DC 20402
(202) 783-3238

Comment: The U.S. Government is an excellent source of information. They offer many publications to help in your business, many free or at small cost.

Product Safety Publications

U.S. Consumer Product Safety Commission
Washington, DC 20207

Comment: Gives you free information on publication lists on product safety.

Patents and Trademarks

U.S. Dept. of Commerce
Patent and Trademark Office
Washington, DC 20231

Comment: The U.S. Government offers booklets on trademarks and patents.

Selling to Government

Office of Business Liaison
U.S. Dept. of Commerce
Washington, DC 20230
(202) 377-3176

Comment: The liaison office acts as an important link between the Department of Commerce and the Small Business community. There are 38 federal information centers in the United States. Look up the local one in your community, in the white pages of your phone book under the U.S. Government.

Exporting/Importing

Department of Commerce Publications
U.S. Government Printing Office
Washington, DC 20402
(202) 783-3238

Comment: Many publications are available from the government on this subject.

Advertising Agencies

Directory of Advertising Agencies
3004 Glenview Rd.
Wilmette, IL 60091

Comment: This directory lists the agencies. Choose an agency based on their experience in mail order. Choose carefully, start as early as possible, use as often as needed. Read the contract carefully before signing.

Outside Consultants

Comment: The same as the advertising agency. Choose an outside consultant with experience in mail order. Make certain of costs before you hire the outside consultant.

Trade Shows

Successful Meetings Magazine
633 Third Ave.
New York, NY 10017

Comment: Monthly publication listing trade shows. Also watch newspapers for announcements of shows or call convention facilities.

Associations

Association Directories

Comment: Check with your local librarian, many libraries have these available in reference sections.

Writing Professionals

Comment: They can help write your advertisements, brochures, sales letter, and news releases. Ask for 2 samples of his/her work, and agree on a price before presenting the work. Available in your telephone book under writing services, or direct marketing.

Artists

Comment: Artists will prepare illustrations of products, layouts, or of printed work. Some artists can design a logo for your company.

Photographers

Comment: Ask for a sample of previous work and get a written quote. A photographer can prepare black and white or color photographs of your product or service.

Accounting/Bookkeeping Help

Comment: Good accounting records are essential for success. If you cannot get help, or handle the books yourself, hire an accountant to set up your books. You can find him/her in the telephone book under accountant.

Magazines, Newspapers, Radio, Television Stations

Standard Rate and Data Publication
3004 Glenview Rd.
Wilmette, IL 60091

Comment: This guide offers you the complete listing and rates for various advertising mediums. Your local library may have a copy of it.

Local Chamber of Commerce or Business Association

Comment: These associations help you meet others in business. Some members are potential customers, as well as friends, and associates. You can find their number in the telephone book.

Labor Statistics

Department of Labor
Washington, DC 20210

Comment: Publishes the monthly labor review, and many statistics, trends, employment updates. Labor statistics are available from your state labor department as well.

Government Census Reports

A. Census of Manufacturers
B. Census of Mineral Industries
C. Census of Retail Trade
D. Census of Wholesale Trade
E. Census of Service Industries
F. Census of Transportation

For more information and ordering procedures, contact:

U.S. Department of Commerce
Bureau of the Census
Washington, DC 20233

Comment: Both A and B are available in printed form, computer tape, or flexible diskettes. Ask for form POF 706 to order. Census C, D, E, and F are available in printed form, computer tape, or flexible diskettes. Ask for Form 696 to order.

Some mail-order owners should consider developing products and services to cater to the service industries.

Mailing Lists

Standard Rate and Data Services Inc.
3004 Glenview Rd.
Wilmette, IL 60091

Comment: This publication offers important information on mailing lists.

Local Library

Comment: Your research librarian can be your best friend, consultant or advisor on where you can get various information, data, publications and services, for your business. Some libraries have computer data banks with other libraries.

Free Telephone Calls

Call 800-555-1212

Comment: Many magazines, companies, and agencies offer free 800 numbers to their customers. Check to see if they have an 800 number before you dial it. Also, ask about telephone directories offered by telephone companies for 800 numbers.

Appendix C

A to Z Promotion Ideas

A. News Releases
B. Prompt replies to inquiries
C. Customer follow-up with new mailing
D. Teaching your favorite subject
E. Speaking to business or professional group
F. Speaking on radio or television show
G. Writing an article on your business in your trade magazine
H. Get some exposure from a newsletter in your mail-order field.
I. Call a customer to answer a question about your product or service.
J. Talk with others in mail order to find new ideas.
K. Swap your list for a list of same or better quality with another mail-order owner.
L. Present your product to other mail-order dealers.
M. Sell your product to large catalog houses.
N. Sell your product to fast-growing market, such as the service industries.
O. Mail out your special offer or newest offer each day. For example, send out at least 50 each day.
P. Join a business organization for contacts and ideas.
Q. Write a letter to the editor about your field of interest. For example, one mail-order owner writes about small business, another about the value of crafts as a hobby.
R. Send postcards to your best customers about upcoming sale and date of new catalog release.

S. Split a mailing with another noncompeting mail-order owner—for example, a gift seller with a lamp seller.
T. Send new offer or catalog in shipping package of latest sale.
U. Put your address and phone number on each sheet of promotional material.
V. Donate your time or a product or service—for example, an educational television station that accepts gifts for auctions to raise money.
W. Tell your best customers often, how much you appreciate and need them.
X. Ask your customers to give you names of friends and associates to whom you can sell. (This could be included in your direct sales package.)
Y. Use testimonials. Nothing sells better than endorsement from others.
Z. Keep selling, selling, and selling.

Index